The 1:1 Roadmap
Setting the Course
for Innovation in Education

To my parents, Rick and Jean, for always

giving me and my brother, Adam, the opportunity

to think differently and

explore our creative passions

The 1:1 Roadmap
Setting the Course
for Innovation in Education

Andrew P. Marcinek

CORWIN
A SAGE Company

A SAGE Company

FOR INFORMATION:

Corwin
A SAGE Company
2455 Teller Road
Thousand Oaks, California 91320
(800) 233-9936
www.corwin.com

SAGE Publications Ltd.
1 Oliver's Yard
55 City Road
London, EC1Y 1SP
United Kingdom

SAGE Publications India Pvt. Ltd.
B 1/I 1 Mohan Cooperative Industrial Area
Mathura Road, New Delhi 110 044
India

SAGE Publications Asia-Pacific Pte. Ltd.
3 Church Street
#10–04 Samsung Hub
Singapore 049483

Executive Editor: Arnis Burvikovs
Associate Editor: Ariel Price
Editorial Assistant: Andrew Olson
Production Editor: Kelly DeRosa
Copy Editor: Terri Lee Paulsen
Typesetter: Hurix Systems Pvt. Ltd.
Proofreader: Theresa Kay
Indexer: Virgil Diodato
Cover Designer: Anupama Krishnan
Marketing Manager: Lisa Lysne

Printed in the United States of America.

A catalog record of this book is available from the Library of Congress.

ISBN: 9781-4522-2634-7

This book is printed on acid-free paper.

SUSTAINABLE FORESTRY INITIATIVE
Certified Chain of Custody
Promoting Sustainable Forestry
www.sfiprogram.org
SFI-01268
SFI label applies to text stock

14 15 16 17 18 10 9 8 7 6 5 4 3 2 1

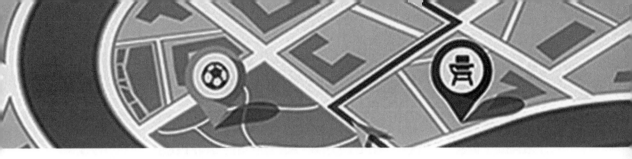

Contents

Acknowledgments

Corwin gratefully acknowledges the following reviewers for their editorial insight and guidance:

Dr. Deborah Alexander-Davis, Educational Consultant; Adjunct Professor
Tennessee Tech University
Cookeville, TN

Sherry Annee, HS Science Teacher
Brebeuf Jesuit Preparatory School
Indianapolis, IN

Robert C. Bennett, Mentor/Coach
FIRST Lego League/FIRST Robotics
Crestwood Middle School/East Kentwood HS
Kentwood, MI

Kathy Benson, Technology Integration Teacher
Vincent Farm Elementary
White Marsh, MD

Regina Brinker, Science Teacher
Christensen Middle School
Livermore, CA

Kathy Ferrell, Instructional Coach
Excelsior Springs Middle School
Excelsior Springs, MO

Carol S. Holzberg, Technology Coordinator
Greenfield Public Schools
Greenfield, MA

John Lustig, District Technology Director
Saint Peter Public Schools
Saint Peter, MN

Dr. Neil MacNeill, Principal
Ellenbrook Independent Primary School
Ellenbrook, WA, Australia

Betsy Muller, Technology Teacher
Cougar Ridge Elementary School
Bellevue, WA

Edward C. Nolan, Instructional Specialist, Mathematics
Montgomery County Public Schools
Rockville, MD

Judith A. Rogers, EdD
K–5 Mathematics Specialist
Tucson Unified School District
Tucson, AZ

Dr. Bonnie Tryon, SAANYS Representative
NY State Education Department's NCLB Committee of Practitioners
New York, NY

Dr. Gary L. Willhite, Professor/Teacher Educator
University of Wisconsin–La Crosse
La Crosse, WI

Margie Zamora, Project Facilitator
Instructional Technology
Clark County School District
Las Vegas, NV

About the Author

Andrew P. Marcinek has experience in combining technology and education, spanning several years inside and outside of the classroom. Most recently he assumed the duties of director of technology at Grafton Public Schools in Grafton, Massachusetts. Prior to that, he served as the director of technology for Groton-Dunstable Regional School District and instructional technology specialist at Burlington High School, both in Massachusetts. Previously, he spent seven years as a secondary English teacher and college professor in Pennsylvania. At Burlington, he played a major role in launching a 1:1 iPad environment, organizing the iPad deployment, and leading several educational technology professional development events in Burlington and Groton-Dunstable Regional School District.

Beyond professional development and the iPad launch at Burlington High School, Andrew has designed and created a digital and information literacy course that focuses on web 2.0 applications, Google Apps for Education, information literacy, and digital citizenship. Similarly, he created, designed, and developed the 1:1 high school student Genius Bar, or help desk, that provides technology support for students and staff.

At Groton-Dunstable Regional School District, Andrew was in charge of a $562,000 grant for technology. In that time, he created a strategic plan that provided a sustainable education technology environment that immediately impacted teaching and learning. Along with the tech team, he transitioned staff and students to Google Apps for Education, provided professional development for the entire staff, launched and managed 700 Google Chromebooks, presented weekly optional after-school professional development for staff, refreshed faculty laptops by providing the choice between Mac and PC, and upgraded the network infrastructure to provide robust, wireless access in all six school buildings.

Outside the classroom, Andrew organized four Edcamps and presented at various conferences around the country. Similarly, he developed community tech nights for both Burlington Public Schools and Groton-Dunstable Regional School District communities. This was a monthly event in the evening that provided a focused EdTech subject and workshop opportunities for anyone in the community. Andrew regularly blogs for Edutopia and consults with school districts on technology initiatives through his company, EducatorU.org.

Introduction

Throughout time, technology has taken on many forms in the classroom. To think, at one time the slate chalkboard was a modern innovation that impacted the classroom along with classroom management. The evolution of the classroom chalkboard draws so many parallels to what I am about to share in this text. Before the chalkboard, students used individual slates, which made instructing the entire class at once impossible for teachers. But

> In 1801, the rather obvious solution to the problem made its debut. James Pillans, headmaster and geography teacher at the Old High School in Edinburgh, Scotland, is credited with inventing the first modern blackboard when he hung a large piece of slate on the classroom wall. In America, the first use of a wall-mounted blackboard occurred at West Point in the classroom of instructor George Baron. (Concordia University, n.d., para. 5)

As generations move from one to the next, we must keep in mind our past, while attending to our present, with our eyes on the future. As an educator, we must embrace and understand our past, present, and future so that we can prepare our students for a world that, for many of us in the classroom, is unfamiliar. In my experience as an aspiring screenwriter, an English teacher, an instructional technology specialist, and most recently, a director of technology, I've had the opportunity to not only work in progressive schools, but with progressive leaders and colleagues. These opportunities have provided me with a story to tell about my firsthand experiences integrating technology.

In the following pages, I am going to share my experience in getting a 1:1 iPad initiative off the ground, supporting the initiative, and fostering a shared culture of learning. This book, while primarily for school leaders, covers classroom practice and classroom management, as well as ways to remix and rethink the standard classroom lesson. Anyone involved in education should continue reading; however, those that will gain the most are school leaders looking to develop a plan to integrate new technologies in order to promote and foster 21st century learning.

This book is not a blueprint for developing a 21st century learning environment, but rather a roadmap that presents a course that you can follow, but it also provides plenty of options for diverging from this course. My purpose for writing this book was to share a unique experience that yielded positive results at two schools. Both environments, completely different, share two perspectives on integrating technology, rethinking instructional design, and providing support for students.

Additionally, this book offers primers for district leaders to prepare their district for a large-or small-scale technology initiative. It offers essential steps to get started and provides ideas for sustaining and supporting this initiative. Also, this text provides practical lessons for teachers and technology specialists. If you work in a school that is already working within a technology initiative, this text will offer ideas that you can immediately put into practice. This work is not device agnostic and represents multiple platforms for integration beyond an iPad.

The perspective is from my direct experience in Burlington Public Schools and Groton-Dunstable Regional School District, in Massachusetts. In both districts, I played a key role in planning and launching large-scale technology initiatives. There are also testimonials from district leaders, students, and teachers who I had the pleasure of working with during both initiatives. Their words provide a glimpse of what the day-to-day, 1:1 school looks like. Their experiences reinforce the assertions I present throughout about digital learning and technology integration. Plus, there is limited focus on actual device specifications and more of a focus on planning strategies and teaching ideas. While devices in this context are important, the focus lies more with the philosophy.

Although the hardware and applications continue to evolve and move at a swift pace, the focus remains—and should always remain—on the learning objectives. In my experience teaching in the secondary classroom, as an instructional technology specialist and as a director of technology, I've always made technology secondary to what I was teaching. Additionally, technology, whether it was hardware or an application, provided access to a wealth of opportunities that I was eager to integrate into my classroom. Challenging students to think, be creative, and explore different pathways of inquiry is just as essential as turning a device on.

In the past ten years the physical K–12 classroom has changed dramatically. While some will argue that someone from 1900 could walk into a contemporary classroom and relate to what is happening, the modern classroom has changed. But how? How is a room that places an autocratic figure at the front of the room, desks in line in the middle, and students all facing in one direction any different? The simple answer is technology.

The fact that the global economy relies on technology daily is one of the many pieces of evidence I will provide for why technology has a place in the classroom. In education, we can no longer look at technology as a "Computer Class," but a literacy that must be threaded throughout the fabric of a school. Today's job demands not only a diverse skill set in technology, but also an employee who can adapt to a myriad of environments. Some of the best companies in the world are employing this type of person right now. In a recent piece in the *New York Times,* Thomas Friedman asked Laszlo Bock, the senior vice president of people operations for Google, what they look for in a candidate:

> "There are five hiring attributes we have across the company," explained Bock. "If it's a technical role, we assess your coding ability, and half the roles in the company are technical roles. For every job, though, the No. 1 thing we look for is general cognitive ability, and it's not I.Q. It's learning ability. It's the ability to process on the fly. It's the ability to pull together disparate bits of information. We assess that using structured behavioral interviews that we validate to make sure they're predictive." (Friedman, 2014)

This is not to say that the goal of every teacher and school is to get their students to someday work for Google, but rather, provide them with challenges in the classroom that elicit a variety of skill sets. And, technology provides that opportunity.

While technology in the classroom is still a new concept, it's one that will never sit still. Many will argue that education technology is simply a fad or a phase. And, while there is some merit in this statement, it's now the job of the school administration team to consistently provide the best, new technology to support students and teachers. In short, technology needs to be treated as if it were oxygen: necessary, invisible, and ubiquitous (Lehmann, 2009). While this book focuses on my experience with a large-scale 1:1 iPad initiative, it's not simply about technology—it's about creating a healthy, challenging learning environment for the 21st century student.

While I could spend days answering questions (many are answered in the following pages) about the impact of technology integration, there is one important question that every school must keep in mind: "Why are we doing this?" This should drive the initial discussion and lead to developing a sustainable plan that ultimately comes down to providing the best access, the best resources, and the best learning opportunities for all students.

The 1:1 Roadmap

- **Why are we integrating technology?**
- **Planning the technology initiative**
- **It's not about the device**

BEGIN WITH THE "WHY?"

While there is no central blueprint for a large-scale 1:1 device launch or Bring Your Own Device (BYOD) initiative in your school, there are several key components that schools should follow. Every school's plan will be different based on size, budget, personnel, and so on. The first question every school must ask itself is *"Why are we doing this?"* While this may seems obvious, it's not as easy to answer as you might think. There's a big difference between a school that "has technology" and a school that "leverages technology to impact teaching and learning and uses data to drive its future purchases and initiatives." Burlington Public Schools Superintendent Eric Conti stated, "We're not integrating a large-scale 1:1 iPad initiative to increase MCAS [Massachusetts Comprehensive Assessment System] scores. We're doing it because students need to understand technology devices as well as digital literacy."

Patrick Larkin, Burlington Public Schools assistant superintendent, in his blog series *Becoming a 1:1 School*[1] elaborates on the "Why?" in relation to "What?" he expects out of education and access to technology as a father of three children:

> As we make the transition to a 1:1 school questions continue to arise in regards to why and how we are doing this . . . and they should.

While the how is important in regards to the allocation of resources in financially difficult times, I believe that if we do a good job answering the why of this question then the how becomes less significant. Before I get started with a few specifics in answering the why, I have a question to ask . . .

. . . What type of education do we want for our kids?

Being a father of three, I have some things that I want for my children:

- I want my children to learn about resources that allow them to connect and collaborate with those who share their passions/interests.
- I want my children to be inquisitive and lead their own learning.
- I want my children to be responsible citizens.

I am bothered by the fact that the world outside of our schools has changed so dramatically, while the world inside has changed very little. It would seem to me that we would start to see changes inside our schools that would correspond to what is happening outside.

It's important to recognize that all of the items Larkin references are not related to a specific device, but rather to a shift in how students learn and what resources both students and teachers have access to.

In my early writings about 1:1 and after experiencing a variety of devices in different environments, I've come away with some driving forces behind the "Why?"

- Access to a vast collection of resources

- Develop 21st century skills and understand digital spaces

- Anytime learning

- Reduce paper and transition to digital workflows

- Provide assistive technology for students

- Promote careers and interest in computer science

- Give teachers tools to remix "stand and deliver" lessons

And I am certain I could go on with this list. However, I did not mention state standardized tests going online. Nor did I mention to increase test scores. I will let you in on a little secret: Devices do not improve standardized test scores. While high-stakes testing is still a major part of the American educational system, devices should not be your change agent for better scores.

INFRASTRUCTURE

Once you've addressed the "Why?," district technology leaders will want to ensure that the wireless infrastructure is adequate. Additionally, technology directors will want to ensure that their budget can support and sustain the infrastructure. This is not to say that wireless access points will need to be replaced yearly, but upgrades and repairs will be something to expect each budget cycle. At Burlington, we turned this category into a line item in the yearly budget. Every year we had an encumbrance for network infrastructure. And that's it. In short, we treat our network infrastructure just as we would treat our heating, water, and electric bills.

Without a robust, stable infrastructure in place, the devices won't work effectively, teachers and students won't be inclined to use technology that's slow and cumbersome, and eventually, the plan will fail. Currently, it is recommended that schools provide a wireless infrastructure that reaches speeds of at least 100 mbs (megabits per second). In two years, President Barack Obama would like schools to employ a 1 gb (gigabit) line. Regardless of the vendor you choose, this piece must not only be installed correctly and effectively, but also maintained by the network managers.

During our iPad launch in 2011, Burlington boasted a 100 mbs bandwidth. At the time, this worked well for our environment, but it was evident from day one of having students in the building that we would need more bandwidth going forward. Initially, we wanted every student in the high school to download the student handbook on the first day of school during advisory. I got on the all-call and announced instructions to the entire school. Before I could get to the part where students clicked on the link, we had choked our network. It was down. Day one of our iPad adventure and we choked the network. Within the hour network managers fixed the problem and the school's network was back up and running. As we went on that year we realized that eventually, in the coming fiscal year, we would need to upgrade our bandwidth. One of our biggest issues was connection to Apple's servers; therefore, we had to throttle this address. In short, students could not download apps on our network during the first year. I mean, they could, but it took forever. We also had to throttle Pandora and other streaming services. The following year we upgraded our bandwidth to 400 mbs and released the throttles on the aforementioned applications.

When districts are pioneering technology initiatives, it's essential to treat the aforementioned story as a learning moment and not a failure. It's imperative to accept that every initiative may not go as planned, but to learn as you go and put forth a tireless effort to make sure the technology initiative moving along in beta is not disrupting the classroom. Ultimately, the technology team and district leaders must have an open line of communication along with a vision that is focused and flexible.

ACCEPTABLE USE POLICY

The Acceptable Use Policy (AUP) is the next phase in this process. In my experience at Burlington Public Schools and Groton-Dunstable Regional School District, we reviewed and updated our AUPs to align with new technology standards, new devices, and new access for students. I recommend reviewing your Acceptable Use Policy once a year and bringing in technology leaders along with administration. Ultimately, the school committee or board will approve the final policy that ends up in your district's policy book. This policy should be very general and serve as an umbrella for building-based procedures that building principals will want to review with technology leaders.

When districts look at their AUPs, they should be aware of providing students and teachers with liberal access to information needed for school while staying within the context of the Children's Internet Privacy Act (CIPA), the Children's Online Privacy Protection Act (COPPA), and the Family Educational Rights and Privacy Act (FERPA). Currently, there are some schools that employ a Responsible Use Policy. The simple change in semantics presents a positive connotation so that students feel more empowered to use technology responsibly, rather than simply what is accepted. Regardless of word choice, this document(s) is the founding piece to ensure your technology initiative is working under the proper, federal guidelines. Below is a revised Acceptable Use Policy that I adapted from the Responsible Use Guidelines created by Forsyth County Schools (2013).

Empowered Digital Use Guidelines

> The mission of the Groton-Dunstable Regional School District (GDRSD) is to prepare and inspire all students to contribute and excel in a connected, global community. The district provides engaging instruction that develops digital citizenship skill sets for using technology as a tool to achieve this mission. Information and Communication Technology is an integral part of GDRS' curriculum across subjects and grades in developmentally appropriate ways, and it is aligned to the competencies listed in the Massachusetts and Common Core State Standards which include: seek knowledge and understanding; think critically and solve problems; listen, communicate and interact effectively; exhibit strong personal qualities; and engage and compete in a global environment.
>
> I understand that using digital devices (whether personal or school owned) and the GDRSD network is a privilege, and when I use them according to the Responsible Use Guidelines I will keep that privilege.
>
> I will:
>
> - Use digital devices, networks and software in school for **educational purposes and activities**.

- Keep my personal information (including home/mobile phone number, mailing address, and user password) and that of others **private**.
- Show **respect** for myself and others when using technology including social media.
- Give **acknowledgement to** others for their ideas and work.
- **Report inappropriate** use of technology immediately.

The Responsible Use Procedure will be reviewed each school year together with students and teachers and will provide a springboard for teaching and learning around topics such as Internet safety, digital citizenship and ethical use of technology.

One of the important elements of this policy is that it covers everything that is related to technology use throughout an organization. It conveys this message in a tone that is nonthreatening and clear to every student, K–12, who reads it. And, while this policy serves as our umbrella policy for the school district, there are also procedural documents that students must sign off on before using our technology. These documents are split up into K–8 and 9–12. They can be found in the Appendix of Resources of this text.

In both situations I served on the AUP revision teams. And in both scenarios students now had access to e-mail through Google Apps for Education organizational accounts. In some old AUP policies the use of e-mail was prohibited during school hours. Now, e-mail is an essential part of communication between teachers and students. In both Burlington and Groton-Dunstable, student e-mail differed slightly from staff e-mail. The first notable difference is the domain. At Groton-Dunstable, the teachers' domain is @gdrsd.org while the students' domain is @gdrsd.us. This distinction was made because student e-mail can only send and receive internally. That means students can technically sign up for a Twitter account with his or her e-mail, but they will not receive the activation e-mail needed to initiate the account. However, the Google Apps administrator can allow domains for students if teachers request it to be allowed. For example, our high school English department uses vocabulary.com. Her students sign up for the site and are sent an e-mail to verify their accounts. In the Google Apps dashboard the Google Apps administrator can add the domain extension "vocabulary .com" so that e-mails will come through to student accounts.

SELECTING A DEVICE

"IT'S NOT ABOUT THE DEVICE, IT'S ABOUT LEARNING GOALS AND OBJECTIVES."

My former colleague Dennis Villano, the director of Instructional Technology at Burlington, coined this phrase when we started deploying and presenting our 1:1

iPad initiative to parents and students. His forethought was spot on. During our initial planning at Burlington, we tested a variety of devices: everything from netbooks, laptops, and the iPad. Coincidentally, it was right around the same time that Apple was getting ready to announce the second iPad. We watched intently and realized from the keynote that the iPad 2, even though it would be uncharted waters, made sense and had potential. The tech team, along with the administrative team, had no idea what to expect, but our minds were already imagining the possibilities with the iPad 2 in the hands of teachers and students.

During the summer of 2011, the Burlington tech team became a cohesive entity under the direction of Villano. With the support of Superintendent Conti and High School Principal Larkin, the tech team was trusted and simply allowed to work. Along with Bob Cunha and Jose DeSousa, district network managers, we began to play. And by "play" I mean we started to explore the potential of this device in the hands of students. Additionally, we started to explore how the iPad 2

- would impact our network bandwidth,

- would be deployed to 1,000 students before the start of school,

- would impact classroom management,

- would impact teachers' lessons,

- would impact students beyond our network and at home,

- would impact printing (since we did not allow printing from the iPads),

- would integrate with our student information system, and

- would integrate with Google Apps for Education.

Villano and I began working on digital workflows and creating a short list of foundational apps for both students and teachers. We also began designing a rollout plan to ensure we could reach every student, parent, or guardian.

We also created a model for summer professional development that will be explored later in this text. But, Villano and I created "Edcamp Tuesdays"[2] over the summer. These days were optional for teachers in our district and beyond. In short, we simply wanted to bring educators together to share ideas and findings around the iPad 2. While these sessions were not packed or overflowing, they were well attended by our teachers and teachers outside of our district who were curious to see where the iPad in education was going. For everyone involved it was a tremendous learning experience and a successful way to provide support and optional professional development throughout the summer months.

Deciding on a device for your school is much different today. At this writing there are a host of options for schools to integrate and at reasonable prices. I've had the pleasure of seeing this evolution from the beginning. My perspective is from both inside the classroom and looking in from afar. What's changed dramatically in the past few years has been schools' ability to integrate robust wireless infrastructure and the cost of software.

As I mentioned before, the device you select should be a collective effort. With the rise of Google's Chromebook and Nexus 7 Android tablets, the iPad now has stiff competition in the educational technology market. Ultimately, selecting a device comes down to several factors that are specific to each school:

1. **Annual Budget**—As I have mentioned before, schools should purchase a device with the replacement in mind. Technology moves quickly, and district leaders should understand that this process must include a plan for sustainability. That is, if we purchase Samsung Chromebooks this year, what will they look like in two years? How will we financially support old devices? Should we support old devices or upgrade to new ones? These are just a few of the questions you'll want to map out before moving forward with a device. Also, it's essential to make sure the devices that are on the table to be selected arrived there through a collaborative effort from teachers, students, parents, and administrators.

2. **Test or Pilot Devices**—Before devices arrive on the table to test, it's a good idea to integrate several of these devices before a decision is made. And not just test the devices, but glean feedback from both students and teachers. How do the devices integrate into the classroom? How well do the students and teachers embrace the device? Eventually, there should be a data collection tool to determine device experience. This can be done in a short survey that asks participants.

3. **What Is Your Capacity?**—Once you've selected a device, you'll want to begin planning your district's capacity for integrating these devices. In short, in what grade will this initiative begin? Will this be a school-by-school 1:1? What classrooms, grades, or schools will have devices this year, and who will receive devices next year? Based on my experience, I suggest starting device initiatives in the middle school as opposed to high school—students are still developing skill sets and are open to trying new operations without the pressures of college admissions.

4. **A Hybrid**—If your committee has come to a stalemate on two devices, that's not a bad thing. A hybrid model can work really well and provides teachers and students with access to a variety of systems. Even though Burlington launched a 1:1 iPad initiative, we still provided Chromebooks in our libraries across the district. At Groton-Dunstable, our primary device is the Chromebook; however, we integrated iPads in every school.

5. **Bring Your Own Device (BYOD)**—Finally, there is a case to be made for a BYOD. A BYOD model puts the financial onus on the parents and students but gives the student a personalized device that works best for his or her learning. If you decide to move in this direction, you'll want to get familiar with a mobile device management system, or MDM. An MDM will allow the network administrator to provide a safe environment for student devices coming on to the school's network. This also allows administrators to push profiles and apps to devices, as well as restrict certain apps.

These steps are good discussion points in your initial team meetings about what direction to move. Again, when we started planning for 1:1 at Burlington many devices were vetted. Initially, netbooks were a favorite, but once Apple announced the iPad 2 and its capabilities, it seemed that this was the direction to go. But, this doesn't mean we stopped thinking at the iPad. Ultimately, we explored Chromebooks, Nexus tablets, Windows surface tablets, and so on. The point here is to consistently vet new devices, check in with surrounding districts that are using devices, and approach technology hardware as a constantly moving piece of your district technology plan.

The other option is the computer lab setup. This setup still has a place in K–12, but static computer labs have become less important in the district technology plan. In both experiences, computer labs were limited to the arts department and digital media classes. These classes required hefty programs and higher processing speeds than most mobile solutions boast at the moment.

There is no perfect device that will transform teaching and learning upon its arrival. Ultimately, it is a device in the hands of an educator and a student that are open to exploring new technologies that enhance teaching and learning. What's more, the device should be selected with the best interest of the teachers and students in mind. District leaders should not choose the device that works best for them, but one for the teachers and students.

Teacher Readiness and Parent Support

Once the tech team and district leaders have squared away the logistics and have selected a device, it's time to develop an integration strategy. This begins with teacher prep. In my experiences at Burlington and Groton-Dunstable, ensuring that teachers across the content areas were prepared was essential to this transition being successful.

However, district leaders must approach technology integration at a healthy pace. The key is trust and transparency. It is also essential to provide time for teachers to acclimate to the devices and applications they will be using in the classroom. At both Burlington and Groton-Dunstable, we integrated pilot devices for trials and feedback, provided teachers with devices over the summer to use and adapt to, and developed optional professional development drop-in sessions over the summer.

Additionally, I created a website that included commonly used digital tools and applications along with videos, scripts, and FAQs for quick access. In short, I made an attempt to develop my own version of Khan Academy[3] for EdTech. This resource[4] was a convenient way for teachers, and really anyone in the world, to learn about new and emerging digital tools.

Aside from professional development, one of the best things we added to support our teachers throughout both districts I was involved in was the creation of a student-run help desk. The student help desk, which will be shared in depth in a later chapter, consisted of high school students who wanted to take an elective that would also serve as a support system for EdTech in the schools. The help desk was staffed with students six out of the seven periods of the day, and both teachers and students could visit it and receive instant support. The help desk also created online resources for students, teachers, and the world. This course is regarded, in my opinion, and the opinions of our tech directors, as one of the greatest benefits of our tech initiatives.

In order to prepare parents, we held summer sessions that we referred to as "iPad Driver's Ed"[5] sessions. These sessions were mandatory for all students who were receiving their iPad during year one of our launch and for incoming freshmen. In short, we briefed parents and students on our policies surrounding the new technology, provided information on insurance for the iPad, and shared applications that students should become familiar with before school started. Typically, we held these sessions during the day, and in the evening at the beginning of August.

Additionally, we held Community Tech Nights[6] in both districts that I was a part of and shared different topics and workshops each month. This event was open to anyone in the community. The event generally lasted an hour and a half and included a brief presentation and was followed by a hands-on learning exercise.

What's important initially during device rollouts is that the support offered does not stop. It must be ongoing and include time for teachers to explore and try these new tools. It's also essential for district leaders to develop an assessment tool to evaluate the technology integration. This data was key and helped provide evidence for future technology initiatives. Plus, the data collected also helped with planning the following year's budget and professional development plans.

Some of the initial questions I developed in both districts covered the broad scope that I was looking to assess. Initially, I started with these questions:

1. What is your instructional design process for integrating technology?

2. How are you using technology to transition learning from a passive experience to an active, creative experience?

3. How have you remixed the physical space and leveraged technology to create active learning experiences?

4. How do you know technology is impacting student learning?

These inciting questions helped me develop and evolve the strategic plan for technology integration throughout the district. After the first year, I parsed these questions down into more specific questions:

1. How would you rate your access to technology devices this year?

2. How often did you integrate technology into your classroom practice?

3. How would you rate your experience with Google Apps for Education?

4. How would you rate your experience with the wireless network in your respective building?

5. How would you rate your experience with accessing digital resources?

6. How would you rate the support for technology throughout the school year?

7. Do you feel the new technology in the district impacted student learning and growth? (Included a text both for respondents to elaborate.)

8. Did the Google Chromebooks provide a reliable, intuitive resource for students in your class?

9. How would you rate your experience using iPads in the classroom?

10. In what areas can the tech team improve? In what ways did the tech team meet or exceed your expectations?

Ultimately, it's important to drive a technology initiative with collective, collaborative input. A technology director should not make decisions that serve his or her comfort zone, but rather, he or she should listen and support technology that will impact teaching and learning. Additionally, district leaders should proceed with a plan that is not simply for one year, but one that can sustain within the parameters of a school's technology budget. Buying new devices and expecting to get 10 years out of them is not practical. While I am certain this practice could be done, it's not a healthy practice. Before devices are even purchased, district leaders should develop a five-year plan for the sustainability of all technology and include periodic upgrades.

The roadmap detailed in this chapter is not the golden ticket to successful technology integration; however, it presents a good menu of options that districts can use to make this transition. What's important is that district leaders constantly keep in mind how the technology will impact the learning. Additionally, it is imperative that districts have a plan beyond year one and can ensure that the technology budget can support upgrades each year. Once you've settled your plan, it's time to start thinking about provoking change in your school. I consider this change a shift in school culture and how we think about 21st century instructional design and practice. The devices and technology plan are phase one; shifting a school culture is what follows.

ENDNOTES

1. http://www.patrickmlarkin.com/p/becoming-11-school-series.html
2. https://sites.google.com/a/bpsk12.0rg/edcamp-tuesdays/home
3. https://www.khanacademy.org/
4. https://sites.google.com/a/gdrsd.org/gdrsd-edtech-commons/
5. http://www.markjsullivan.org/2011/08/ipad-distribution-for-1000-students.html
6. http://gdrsdedtech.org/2014/03/10/march-community-tech-night-313/

A Cultural Shift

- Cultivating a cultural shift in your school
- Devices provoke change
- Innovation begins with trust

Figure 2.1 shows the levels of trust between all stakeholders within a school district. The arrows between titles indicate that trust must be a two-way street and that from top to bottom all members of a school district team must trust in each other's decisions and embrace constructive criticism. The other component that helps develop trust is listening and embracing all sides before moving forward. In education, top-down leadership is not the way to proceed.

Aside from trust, there needs to be consistent conversations, not essentially meetings, about new and emerging initiatives. These conversations include all stakeholders and should be a driving force in providing the best opportunities and access for all members of a school district.

At both Burlington and Groton-Dunstable, I regularly met with district leaders, principals, teachers, and students. These interactions were mostly informal but yielded a productive dialogue that resulted in first-hand feedback for various technology initiatives. The best advice for these interactions is to listen. When I arrived at Groton-Dunstable as the director of technology, I spent weeks listening, assessing the technology, and meeting with teachers in classrooms. I also shared these experiences with the Groton-Dunstable tech team weekly during our tech team meetings. This formula was helpful for all involved, and it provided excellent feedback. Additionally, it unclogged the hierarchy pipeline and provided an opportunity for conversation and trust across all levels of the school district.

FIGURE 2.1 The Pathway to Trust
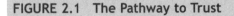

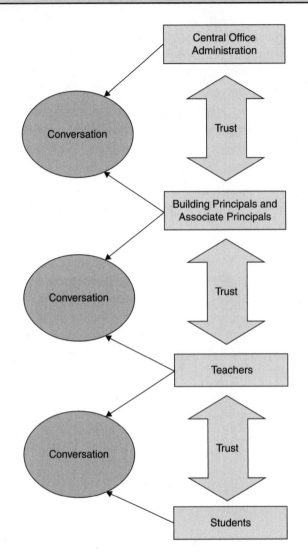

The more I work with schools that are seeking device integration, the more I stress the importance of developing a school culture around those devices. I've seen technology initiatives falter or lose momentum when devices suddenly appeared and magic was expected to happen. If you're searching for evidence here, look no further than LA Unified School District.

LA Schools Superintendent John Deasy has called the intended $1 billion program to provide an iPad to every student in the district a civil rights imperative with potential to equalize access to technology. But the initiative, the largest of its kind, stumbled this fall during its first phase—a $30 million rollout to 47 schools—after some 300 high school students skirted the tablets' security to surf social-networking sites.

Under pressure, Deasy called for a delay of the rollout, which means all schools aren't likely to get the devices until 2015—a year later than planned. (Iasevoli, 2013)

What's more, we cannot expect students and teachers to simply adapt to technology because it's the 21st century and Twitter says so. The pace at which we integrate technology is equally as important as our developing a positive school culture around technology.

> In Miami, assistant superintendent Sylvia Diaz says her district decided to follow San Diego's example, where it took six years to get a device into the hands of each student.
>
> "We're going to take baby steps and get this right," says Diaz. Miami-Dade has a few small mobile technology programs up and running in the district already. The most recent plan is to hand out devices to seventh and ninth-graders for use in social studies classes. If the program is a success, it will be expanded to other grades and subjects.
>
> For any new program to work, teachers need professional development and technical support, she said. The district this week announced that it will equip all classrooms with a digital science curriculum and provide training for teachers on how to use it.
>
> Above all, Diaz stresses the importance of making sure the instructional purpose of using iPads is clear—an issue that has gotten lost amid LA's messy rollout.
>
> "It's really about asking, 'Why are we doing this?'" Diaz said. (Iasevoli, 2013)

Technology can be a great addition to any school, but it can also be a logistical nightmare if added too quickly and not planned effectively. In my experience of consulting with school leaders, working in the classroom, and designing several large-scale technology initiatives, I've learned many pieces of this puzzle. In this chapter, I'll outline three important issues that every school leader should consider before devices enter the school. I'll also discuss how to sustain this momentum through remixing your faculty meetings and professional development.

Develop a Culture of Trust and Openness

Every districtwide and building-based administrator should develop a strong relationship with his or her technology director and network manager. Additionally, school administration should seek out tech directors who not only understand the server room, but who can also be empathetic and understanding about what classroom teachers need. This is key.

Furthermore, school leaders should place their trust in both teachers and students to leverage the technology in a positive manner. Many times this hasn't been the case, and the school's access is locked down. Instead of locking down the network, open it up and provide opportunities to educate both students and teachers on how this tool should be leveraged in an educational context.

During my work in Burlington Public Schools and Groton-Dunstable Regional School District, I saw this take place first hand. Patrick Larkin, assistant superintendent of learning for Burlington Public Schools and principal during the iPad launch in 2011, exemplified this mindset when he helped transition the high school to a 1:1 iPad environment. Larkin notes that,

> I tried to be transparent with every aspect of the initiative. It certainly helped to have an implementation team comprised of students, teachers, and administrators to help drive the decision-making. (P. Larkin, personal communication, May 14, 2014)

Throughout the initial phases of the 1:1 iPad launch, Larkin and Superintendent Eric Conti leveraged blogs to share their work and quickly update and communicate with the Burlington community. Both Conti and Larkin also took to Twitter to not only learn how other schools were progressing with technology initiatives, but also to share the Burlington initiative. In short, the entire 1:1 transition plan was available and accessible to anyone who wanted to see it. What's more, both Conti and Larkin led the way transparently and placed every detail of the 1:1 transition online for the world to see.[1]

Ultimately, technology should not get in the way of or inhibit classroom practice. This kind of obstruction will happen when districts deploy a technology initiative and attempt to control every last detail about it. While parents have every right to expect caution and transparency from the school district, all parties should also understand that tech integration must proceed with open minds about providing students with access to content and opportunities.

At my current district, Groton-Dunstable Regional School District, I took on the task of revising our Acceptable Use Policy and Access Policies. The first thing I did was develop a new term: Empowered Digital Use Guidelines. The reason behind this change falls in line with my philosophy of education technology, and that is to provide open access to digital resources while working within the parameters of the Children's Internet Privacy Act (CIPA) and the Children's Online Privacy Protection Act (COPPA). Our new policy was molded after a great resource constructed by the Forsyth County Schools Instructional Technology team.

Forsyth County Schools created Responsible Use Guidelines for students, and it consists of one page. After researching their work and reviewing CIPA and COPPA guidelines, I constructed the Empowered Digital Use Guidelines for Groton-Dunstable. This new set of guidelines is simple, clear, and sends a message to students that we're not Big Brother, always looking at their every online move; rather, we are empowering them with technology and digital access so that they can thrive in their learning.

EMBRACE RISK AND PROMOTE INNOVATIVE PRACTICE

This piece comes directly from the building principal and how he or she approaches staff evaluations. With the added pressure of high-stakes testing and emerging models of teacher evaluations, it's challenging for teachers to move too far outside the lines. And, despite the state or federal mandates, administrators should develop an environment that promotes risk taking in the classroom.

When conducting classroom observations, reassure teachers that it's OK if the Wi-Fi drops or the projector cuts out. Ultimately, the focus should be on the content delivery and methodology. Also, understand that the classrooms integrating technology are not always arranged in rows where kids are sitting silently and listening. More often than not, classrooms that are leveraging EdTech are in motion or exhibiting organized chaos. Essentially, contemporary classrooms should resemble a Silicon Valley tech startup. I will discuss some lessons I used to create these models in later chapters.

Don't focus so much on the devices being used in the class, but more importantly on the process toward the learning goals or objectives. Ask students what they're learning, not how they like learning on an iPad. When I observe classrooms, I like to see and hear learning taking place. I am not so much focused on a singular device or an app. Instead, focus on these questions:

- Are the students engaged (beyond simple screen time observations)?

- Is inquiry driving the lesson?

- Is every student working to capacity?

- Will there be evidence of student growth and learning?

DEVICES PROVOKE CHANGE

In my experience I have witnessed many new technologies enter the classroom. These phases bring a subversive, unintended change in how teachers approach classroom management and instruction. The most important element in this shift is trust. It cannot be said enough how important it is for administrators and teachers to trust one another and to trust the students they serve.

Three years ago when I helped launch one of the largest iPad deployments in the country, at Burlington Public Schools, we were still considering technology as a class. Students took a computer class, and teachers took students to the library or computer lab to work on projects. The structure remained intact.

The aforementioned paradigm quickly changed when the iPads touched the hands of every student and teacher in the high school. The physical space no longer mattered. Actually it did, but the necessity beyond the basic needs of heat, water, and network were not that prominent. This is not to say that the iPad took the place of great teaching; however, it did provoke a shift toward project-based and challenge-based learning structures. The content shifted gently, but the big shift came with classroom design and classroom management.

One of the biggest changes during our first year was the phasing out of the traditional language lab used by the Foreign Language Department. The Foreign Language Department chair, Rita DeBellis, decided this space was no longer necessary. The iPad was now a mobile language lab, and every student had access to it no matter where they were. Plus, the Foreign Language Department got approval from the College Board to use the iPad on the AP exam (Shearer, 2012). This was one of the first big shifts that we saw collectively. And it began to shake up tradition across the board.

Spanish teacher Abigail Abbott integrated the iPad exclusively for her classroom instruction. Abbott stopped using the traditional textbook and shifted toward open educational resources, or OER, to supplement the static textbook. She also relied heavily on an app called ShowMe. ShowMe is an interactive whiteboard app that allows users to create and record a presentation using the whiteboard as the canvas. Users can create, record, and post their "ShowMes" either privately or publicly. What Abbott did was use this simple tool to provide anytime, anywhere lessons for her students. Abbott would record a ShowMe[2] and assign it for homework. The next day, students would come in and discuss the contents of the ShowMe that Abbott assigned that night. This shift was not major, but subtle. It required an open mind and a brief challenge to try something new. The technology provoked the change and, in turn, created a classroom where students enjoyed coming.

In a later chapter, I will discuss the professional development aspect of this change as well. It is no secret, as with anything new, some will gravitate immediately, while some will wait and see. Regardless of the pace, it is essential to provide continuous support for any initiative that you put forward.

INNOVATION BEGINS WITH TRUST

When we deployed over 1,000 iPads to teachers and students in the fall of 2011, the tech team along with the administration met several times to discuss the plan. One of the first steps was creating a collective that we could glean ideas from and engage all stakeholders in the Burlington educational community. This team consisted of parents, students, teachers, administration, tech support, and so on. The goal was to present an initiative and get feedback from those who would be involved daily (see Figure 2.2). The results helped greatly in sustaining and keeping our initiative fresh and acceptable for all users.

In preparation for any type of deployment you always want to make sure you have a reliable, robust infrastructure in place. Before we could even begin thinking about

FIGURE 2.2   Technology Advisory Committee Structure

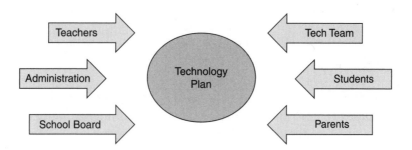

devices we had to consider what type of infrastructure would be supporting it. Once your planning team has checked this item off, you can begin to plan your devices, number of devices, and integration strategies.

One of the best decisions the tech team made when planning our deployment strategy was to include students. We planned a course that, to our knowledge, had never been taught before. The course would simply be called "Help Desk." The model came from Apple's Genius Bar and required students to do more than just adjust the Wi-Fi on a device. I'll discuss this course in more detail later in the book. The point is that we not only solicited information from our students, but we trusted them to assist us in supporting and preparing this launch.

Figure 2.3 shows the process for students who wanted to enter this course. I will dive into the course further in chapter 5, but this was our initial process. This process helped us find students who were not only passionate about technology, but who also demonstrated a desire for complex problem solving, challenge-based learning, self-directed learning, and presentations. We also wanted students who, when faced with a tough situation with their peers (e.g., student hacking an iPad), we could trust to make the right decision.

Our questions varied for each student who came in for an interview. Some examples include these scenarios:

- If you encountered a group of students "jailbreaking" an iPad, what would your response be?

FIGURE 2.3   The Help Desk Interview Process

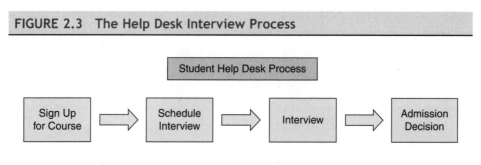

- If you were called to a classroom to fix a projector issue, and after tinkering with it for several minutes the issue was not resolved, what would be your next course of action?

- Briefly describe what it means to be a self-directed learner and provide one personal example of this learning style.

- Describe any experience you've had with customer service. Additionally, describe a moment when you encountered a negative customer. How did you handle this situation?

- What do you hope to accomplish by taking this course? And what skill sets do you anticipate learning or developing?

Aside from the questions, we provided each student with a short demonstrative piece in which they had to address and assess a problem on the spot. Each student encountered three problems, or non-problems, and provided us with a brief assessment of how they solved the issue or how they would proceed. Some of these issues included:

- Student was handed an iPad that could not connect to a Wi-Fi network.

- Student was handed a Chromebook with no battery life.

- Student was handed an iPad that had been "jailbroken."

Once we completed the interview, we allowed students time to ask questions and make comments about the process. Ultimately, the Help Desk class was not a full course load and usually peaked at 10 students per section. However, the support provided throughout the district was invaluable.

In both of my experiences launching a large-scale device initiative—1,000 iPads at Burlington High School and 700 Chromebooks and 200 iPads at Groton-Dunstable Regional School District—I, along with the team, focused on not over-thinking the entire rollout. It's easy to imagine all that could go wrong with any new plan. However, if you lead that way, you'll never get anywhere. The greatest innovators took calculated risks and moved forward despite society or cultural hesitations.

One area that still needs help is in trusting our students. The model has always been to keep the students (workers) in line and ensure that the outcomes are consistent and acceptable. Sound familiar? That formula has been a consistent thread in the school system dating back to its earliest incarnation. Teachers stood in front of the room as the autocratic ruler. Students fell in line and did what they were told or they would earn poor conduct marks. This was, and somewhat still is, how school functions. It was the guiding force in shaping the industrial revolution and bringing about a workforce that was trained to mimic and memorize throughout much of the 19th and early 20th centuries.

This was also the system that great innovators like John Lennon, Bill Gates, Steve Jobs, and Mark Zuckerberg rebelled against. And they all won. Furthermore, what does that say about our educational system if some of the greatest innovators of the 20th century dismissed the standardized educational system and decided to tinker, experiment, and play instead? It says we need to quickly adjust and rethink the way we educate and design instruction—not so much in the content and the fundamental skills students need to learn, but rather in how we deliver this content. This is essential to provoking change in American education. What's more, simply adding access and opportunities to access digital content through devices will help provoke and lead this kind of change.

When we launched our iPad initiative at Burlington High School, the transition did not take place in the course of one year. In fact, it started several years before that with the progressive administration of Superintendent Conti and Principal Larkin. With the support of Conti, one of Larkin's first changes was to allow students to carry cell phones throughout the building. While at this writing this seems like a novel concept, it was the first ripple of what was to come in the area of technology integration. Students could use cell phones in school, but not during classroom time.

> The associate principals would spend the majority of their day chasing down kids to return or solicit their cell phones. It was a waste of their professional time. What's more it was the old guard fighting against the inevitable change. (P. Larkin, personal communication, May 14, 2014)

There are two ways in which you can look at this situation.

1. Continue to fight against advances in technology because you don't understand them and therefore feel insecure about change.

2. Accept that change in education is a constant and should be embraced and developed to ensure all students have access and opportunities to learn, explore, question, and create.

We would assume that most would say their respective schools embrace number two; however, this is not entirely true. In my experience I have seen a blend of both. The simple point is that in order to give our students the best learning opportunities available, we must embrace number two. Additionally, schools must embrace number two if they want to live up to the mission statement that is emblazoned on the front of every school building.

Another glowing example of embracing a culture of trust comes from Michelle Luhtala, head librarian at New Canaan High School (NCHS) in New Canaan, CT. I connected with Luhtala when we were launching our iPad initiative and during a session at Edcamp Boston, where some of her students were on hand to present their shift in thinking about trusting and empowering students with technology. I had the opportunity to speak with her about her program on several occasions. Below is a transcript of how the cultural shift happened at New Canaan High School.

It evolved organically. We unblocked Facebook in 2006 because students found their way around the filter, and we decided it was easier to unblock it and use it for instruction than prohibit its use. We never blocked Twitter or YouTube.

We never prohibited mobile phone use. They've always been allowed [AUP draft in Appendix of Resources]. Whether they are used in class or not is up to the teacher. Sometimes, it is easier to have students use their phones than reserve computers or iPads. Students without smartphones can borrow iPods from the library. We just purchased iPhone 5 keyboards, which we will be circulating from the library. (M. Luhtala, personal communication, May 14, 2014)

The key in this shift is to trust the students and to realize that the more you block and restrict, the more they'll figure it out. Instead of blocking and restricting, educate and leverage these tools that kids are engaged with daily. Consider all of the major shifts that took place over time in education and think about how silly some of them seem to a contemporary teacher. There was actually a time where books were being banned in schools—most notably, *The Catcher in the Rye* (*The Hunger Games* reaches another milestone, 2014).

A few years ago, Winnie Hu tackled this subject in a *New York Times* article titled, "A Call for Opening Up Web Access at Schools." In this article, Hu connected with school librarians, students, and teachers to discuss the positive impact of open access as opposed to all that could go wrong. The article highlights the positive outcomes that students and teachers experience when schools promote trust and openness. According to the article, one librarian encourages his students

To wrestle with the thornier issues of censorship. He asked his students to consider whether schools should block sites espousing neo-Nazi or racist ideas. "It makes them think about it in deeper ways than if they were just to say, 'No, don't block it,'" he said. (Hu, 2011)

And there is more evidence to support this movement toward open access in schools. Luhtala connected with many former students and simply asked them how New Canaan High School prepared them for college and beyond. Here is the question she posted on Facebook to NCHS alumnus along with the responses.

Do you feel that your NCHS education prepared you well for 21st Century citizenship? Did we teach you to be creative, collaborative, respectful, and reflective? Did we teach you to make sound decisions, to publish your work to the world, and to be a participatory learner? If yes, please post comments below.

Katherine Moncure Yes, I definitely think NCHS prepared me for all of these things, especially in regards to active participation and collaboration. In college I was surprised to see just how much other students are used to learning passively and how well NCHS got me in the habit of doing otherwise.

Source: Facebook.com/Katherine Moncure

Similarly, two former students at Burlington Public Schools, who are now in college, also took a moment to reflect on their experience in a progressive high school system that provided access to technology and digital resources. Nick Desimone (class of 2012) stated,

> Going one to one helped to prepare me for not only the next level of education but also beyond that. It helped me understand the consequences of posting garbage on social media. Having an iPad in class and for homework made my educational experience more independent and reflected what I have had in college more than the traditional high school experience did.

Class of 2013 graduate Chris Coe reflected on how this type of access contributed to his learning and work at the next level:

> I had the pleasure of attending Burlington High School just as they began to adopt and nurture a more progressive educational model. With the school's push for technological integration though their 1:1 computing task force, I felt I was being taught more relevant skills for the world I was heading into. Learning to become technologically literate and aware of my digital citizenship has undoubtedly aided me in my college career. The education model, which BHS is continuing to pursue, is working—providing its graduates with a skill set fine-tuned to the future.

While these former students are feeling the impact of progressive technology initiatives, the students currently in school are experiencing the impact of new technologies. Most recently, I spoke with students in the Groton-Dunstable Regional School District and asked them how new technologies integrated this year were impacting their learning.

Regardless of the device we integrate, we must establish a healthy school culture around transparency and trust. Additionally, the impact on student learning is happening with current and graduated students. This culture starts with visionary, progressive leadership. An impactful school leader cannot simply lead alone, but must ensure that there is a dynamic team in place. The goal of this team should be to consistently support teaching and learning and strive every day to make an impact. School leaders must also embrace a culture of trust and open access to resources for learning and inquiry. It is imperative that we provide our students and teachers with access to the best educational and instructional resources

BY AUDREY M.

I'm a seventh grade student at Groton Dunstable Middle School, and the new Chromebooks and use of other technology have really improved our school.

The new Chromebooks are a lot faster than the old laptops, and are smaller and easier to move around the school. Now whenever we are working on a project online, students using the Chromebooks can spend less time waiting for the computers to load and more time working. The Chromebooks are also very easy and simple to use, so you can focus on your work instead of figuring out the technology.

Along with using the Chromebooks, each student received a school email address and a Google Drive account. Before having these email addresses, if a student forgot their homework or couldn't print a paper for some reason, their teachers would have no idea about it and couldn't help the student out. Now, we can email the teachers and get the assignment from them to be ready for class the next day.

Teachers don't have to worry about students losing their papers either because it's all online. With Google Drive you can share your work with others, so teachers and fellow classmates can add comments or help edit your paper. This also means teachers can access their student's work quickly and easily. They can offer ways to improve your assignment in a more efficient way. When students open their Chromebooks they can quickly see their teacher's criticism and fix whatever needs fixing.

For example, in Science class we recently had to write a lab report on an experiment we had done in class. Our teacher brought in the Chromebooks and we used them to type our reports on Google Drive. It was a lot easier than handwriting it or having to type it at home, because we could work on it during class using the Chromebooks and share it with our classmates and teacher through Google Drive to help each other with improving our work. Also our teacher could just look online when they were due and have everyone's reports right there to grade and not have to look for students' lost or late papers.

The use of the new Chromebooks and other technology, like the Google Drive accounts, has benefitted both the teachers and students at our middle school.

available. It's equally important that school leaders embrace trust and allow educators to leverage applications and websites that are familiar to the contemporary student. I'll close this chapter and reinforce its points with a quote from Dennis Villano, who reflects on the importance of providing students with equitable access to technology:

> Our 1:1 iPad initiative has helped our students connect to the world and interact with teachers in ways that were once not possible. These connections have often provided opportunities that could never have happened without the 1:1 program. These untended benefits have impacted student learning and more importantly have helped students grow as people. We have had students organize and lead events, teach professional development sessions to our staff, and work collaboratively with companies on products and applications. While these opportunities may not be recognized by a test score or standardized assessment, they are powerful examples of what a successful technology initiative can provide for students. (D. Villano, personal communication, May 30, 2014)

Developing a healthy, progressive school culture is an essential step in any large- or small-scale technology initiative. School leaders must appropriately pace the technology integration and model digital learning strategies while being transparent and sharing the process. Similarly, school leaders should leverage professional development time to include opportunities for teachers to connect, explore, and share their learning. Professional development ideas will be discussed at length in a later chapter. Also, there should be options throughout the year for teachers to seek out new applications and have time to tinker with them. When these leadership pieces are synthesized with devices and dynamic teachers, we can expect engaging digital learning opportunities to flourish.

ENDNOTES

1. http://www.patrickmlarkin.com/p/becoming-11-school-series.html
2. http://www.showme.com/srtaabbott

3

Cultivating Healthy, Responsible Networks

- **Understanding federal privacy and Internet policies**
- **Digital health and wellness for students using technology**
- **Educating the whole community**

One of the first steps in creating a culture of trust is to allow students access to information. I've encountered many schools that feel it is necessary to block all social media, Google apps, and so on. For the record, there is no law on the books saying that a high school needs to ban all social media and lock down communication avenues and information pipelines. However, it is equally important for schools to educate students about these topics before redacting all of it. A good place to start is a wiki created by Dr. Wesley Fryer called "Unmasking the Digital Truth." This wiki breaks down the lofty verbiage of various federal laws into novice terms.

For example, if you asked most teachers or administrators to summarize the Children's Internet Protection Act, it might be difficult. However, if you use Dr. Fryer's site, you might get a better understanding when you see the language below:

In the United States, schools and libraries receiving federal E-Rate funding are required to provide a basic level of content filtering for their organizational users accessing the Internet. E-Rate was established by the Telecommunications Act of 1996. The Children's Internet Protection Act (CIPA) took effect in 2000. Whether or not an organization is in the United States and is bound by E-Rate requirements and CIPA, content filtering is often used in schools to restrict user access to specific websites or entire categories of websites. Terminology here is interesting: "censorware" is used by some groups and advocates to describe software, hardware, and technology methods which block user access to entire categories or classes of websites. "Blacklist" is the term for the procedure of blocking access to a specific website. "Whitelisting" is a term for the procedure of unblocking or permitting access to specific website(s). In 2006 the "Deleting Online Predators" (DOPA) act was proposed (but defeated) in the U.S. Congress which would have extended CIPA to cover social networking websites.

How do some school administrators invoke CIPA to block web 2.0 sites?

Some school administrators cite CIPA as the reason websites like blogs, wikis, social networking sites, and other sites which permit online communication and collaboration must be blocked.

What does CIPA require?

Citing the text of the law, the *English WikiPedia* reveals:

> CIPA requires schools and libraries using E-Rate discounts to operate "a technology protection measure with respect to any of its computers with Internet access that protects against access through such computers to visual depictions that are obscene, child pornography, or harmful to minors . . ."

CIPA requires E-Rate participating schools and libraries to have a content filtering policy and enforce it.

CIPA does not:

- require specific websites be blocked (sites which are obscene, include child pornography, or are harmful to minors must be blocked)
- require that web 2.0 sites be blocked in general (as a "class" or "category" of websites)
- require that all blog sites be blocked
- require that all wiki sites be blocked
- require that shopping websites be blocked
- require that chat room sites be blocked
- require that Twitter be blocked
- require that all Ning sites be blocked
- require that all social networking websites be blocked
- require that all webmail sites be blocked

- require that Hotmail be blocked
- require that Google Mail be blocked
- require that Yahoo Mail be blocked
- require that instant messaging software programs and websites be blocked
- require that Skype be blocked
- require that iChat be blocked
- require that Internet-capable smartphones be banned at school

What is the takeaway here?

If a school administrator invokes CIPA as the reason for a website to be blocked, and that site does not fall into the category of being "obscene, child pornography, or harmful to minors" then their claim is not legitimate. (CIPA, n.d.)

Source: http://unmaskdigitaltruth.pbworks.com/w/page/7254086/cipa

This starts in kindergarten and threads its way throughout the K–12 curriculum. Students should not be learning about appropriate and fair use online in ninth grade, but they need to develop these skills earlier and gradually understand the positives and negatives of the digital world. This starts with digital health and wellness lessons.

I've written and taught about digital citizenship for several years. And, while the term is new in our lexicon, the meaning spans generations. The simple acts of carrying oneself in a civil, appropriate manner are skill sets that have been integrated into every classroom since the beginning of school. Many would argue that digital citizenship is simply a buzzword and nothing dramatically new. While the underlying meaning is not new, the medium by which adults and students interact has changed dramatically.

Teaching digital citizenship is a fairly new category in the student course list. In the past, students were taught to be civil and work toward being an impactful citizen in one's society. The principle is entwined in many school mission statements as well. In the past, the idea of bullying, teasing, and fighting were seen as "child-like" behavior and addressed as necessary. Students were told at an early age to play nicely together, to share, and not to call each other names. While these events still happened, they did not have the reach and appeal of today.

With the launch of data networks, almost ubiquitous Wi-Fi, and the smartphone, both adults and students alike now share a platform for consuming information and authoring information like our society has never seen. Today's networked society gives everyone a voice, a digital space, a bullhorn to be heard. While this freedom of expression is nothing new to our society, once again it's the medium that's taking it into uncharted territory.

So how do we integrate standards and skill sets that prepare our students, K–12, for an interconnected, digital world that can often be incendiary and hurtful? The unfortunate answer is that we are already behind and too late in some regards. Applications and the pace of technology have outpaced our ability as parents and teachers to keep up with what our students can access.

However, this is not to say we cannot do anything to teach proper digital health and wellness skills for all of our students. One of the key issues is teaching kids offline before they jump into an online world. Kids need to know the harsh realities of a networked world and be able to discern between their offline personality and creating an online personality—and, that both personalities should be the same. Students, at the youngest age, still need to know how to play nicely together, to share, and to not tease or say hurtful things to someone, and they need to be able to transfer those offline skills to a digital space as well. Students need to know the difference between calling someone a name offline and what it would mean if they did the same thing online. In short, students should understand that there should be no difference between the ways they act online in comparison to how they act offline.

Here are some quick ideas for integrating these basic skills sets into the elementary grades:

- Have students write a letter to each other and then to someone beyond the school. This reinforces the transferable skill of writing offline to writing online. This is a great way of introducing e-mail and understanding that the digital world also speaks English and uses the conventions and formatting of proper grammar.

- Have students create something on a large easel paper—this can be a drawing, a poem, a short sentence, and so on. Once completed, have students walk around the room as if they were in a museum and make comments on each creation. This is a great way of having students comment in public and provide authentic feedback that is constructive and not hurtful.

A great resource for the bullet points above is Common Sense Media. Common Sense Media has created K–12 resources, unit plans, and lesson plans. What's great about Common Sense Media resources is that they are accessible, vetted, and practical for teachers to integrate across all the K–12 content areas. Below is an example lesson that addresses the first bullet point mentioned above. It introduces students to a very novel term and sets a good pace for introducing e-mail to elementary students.

Digital spaces should not be painted as all dark and negative, either. Students should understand that great opportunities could now come their way by constructing and maintaining a positive digital presence. When students arrive into the middle school grades they should be able to

DEFINE the Key Vocabulary term **message**.

ASK: *To whom do you send messages? Who sends messages to you?* Encourage students to think about relatives who may live far away, as well as friends from school that they sometimes talk to when they are at home.

ASK: *What kinds of messages do you need to send other people?* Students may mention making plans, sharing news, talking about homework, or wishing someone a happy birthday.

ASK: *What are some ways that you send and receive messages?* You may wish to reinforce students' understanding of the terms "send" and "receive" by writing a short message on a piece of paper and having them pass it around the classroom. They can practice saying the words "send" and "receive" as they hand off the message. Sample responses:

- Written notes passed by hand
- Written letters sent through the mail
- Telephone calls
- Cell phone calls
- Text messages

ASK:

- Have you heard of email?
- Do you have an email account?
- Do other members of your family have an email account?
- Have you ever sent or received an email?
- How do you think email works?

DEFINE the Key Vocabulary term **email**, and encourage students to discuss the idea that email is one way to send and receive messages. (Sending email [K-2], n.d.)

Source: Copyright Common Sense Media, 2014

- generate safe usernames;

- discuss the difference between personal and private information;

- explain why there are logins and passwords on some pieces of hardware, software, and websites;

- describe why stealing information and things others have created is the same as stealing tangible items;

- use technology to explore personal interests; and

- demonstrate to others how to use technology tools in ways that assist learning rather than prevent learning.

Dan Callahan, instructional technology specialist, and Laura D'Elia, school librarian, from Pine Glen Elementary School in Burlington, MA, have a great approach to addressing digital citizenship for elementary students—not to mention, they have a pretty amazing resource that they share from their Pine Glen Library and Technology Center blog.

Both Callahan and D'Elia meshed their respective disciplines together in order to provide students with both information literacy and digital literacy skill sets.

> "Part of a school library curriculum is digital citizenship and it's also part of a technology curriculum and it's one of the reasons why Dan and I have a combined library technology program because we have so many overlaps in our standards and our curriculum."[1]

This model developed by Callahan and D'Elia focuses on two very important elements in the life of a digital citizen: Students should learn not only how to act online, but how to find credible information, and students should also understand how to confront cyberbullying and uncomfortable encounters. These skills can be threaded throughout the curriculum and the content areas. What's more, students should not feel like they have to fall in line with a litany of rigid rules that aim to restrict digital exploration. Students should feel empowered and confident online, but also know that they are safe and secure.

> "I don't think we focus on things to avoid online as much as we focus on what you should be doing online."

What's important to note is that these policies and integration strategies are not the only solution, but rather, they were generated through a collaborative effort of tech team colleagues at both Burlington Public Schools and Groton-Dunstable Regional School District. It offers a good foundation of what students at the elementary level should be expected to know as they move up to middle school. As students grow and climb through the grade levels, these skill sets increase. Once in middle school, students should begin to understand

- how to gather research both online and offline,

- how to interact within digital spaces (such as a Google Doc, Google Site, or Edmodo LMS),

- how to properly find and cite digital media (creative commons, Google Docs research tool), and

- how to discern between positive and negative use of digital spaces and the consequences inappropriate behavior can have.

Julie Spang, instructional technology specialist at Groton-Dunstable Regional Middle School, addresses works collaboratively with many teachers on classroom projects that integrate technology. Spang's initial focus is on how the technology will impact the student learning. Part of that focus relies heavily on digital citizenship.

By the time students get to secondary grade levels, it should be expected that they are exhibiting positive and consistent digital citizenship skills. I've always liked the idea that students graduating to high school should have to pass a digital citizenship driver's education course. This test would demonstrate understanding of the basic standards of what it means to be a digital citizen. At schools that employ 1:1 programs, this would be a good way of obtaining the keys to your device. At Burlington, we made sure every student and parent met with the administration and tech team over the summer (usually during scheduled days in August) to sign and understand our Acceptable Use Policy, get a brief presentation on our systems and the parameters that we created, and to ask questions.

While we, as educators and parents, can make the best efforts to educate our students on digital health and wellness skills, we know that some may slip through the cracks. You can tell a classroom of 30 students to always look both ways before you cross the street, but one out of that 30 will always run without looking. In my experience creating and teaching a digital literacy course,[2] I've seen this come true too many times. The point of this post is that we must continue our mission of educating students not solely on academic merits, but on ethical merits as well. Promote and model good uses of digital spaces in your classroom and in your school. Building a culture of digital health and wellness across a school district will ensure that our students carry out the missions that we have posted on our walls.

BUILDING CLASSROOM COMMUNITY

There's no denying that most of us are engrossed daily with technology. The attachment is evident in most public places. Mobile devices, for most of us, have become our closest friend. In April, the *Telegraph* reported on toddlers becoming so addicted to their iPads that they required therapy.

> She told me she had developed an obsession with the device and would ask for it constantly. She was using it three to four hours every day and showed increased agitation if it was removed. (Ward, 2014)

While this is an extreme case, it's not too far from reality. The mobile device has become our community hub. It's where we go for information and to socialize. It's the new water cooler. In short, our most intimate relationship is with a machine.

In my observations both inside and outside the classroom, I've noticed the relationship with the device to be the most prevalent. This is not to say that teachers are no longer connecting with students, but the devices seem to take precedent. Walk down any city street or attend any event and you'll notice this intimate relationship taking place—head tilted down and thumbs vigorously moving. Shelly Turkle highlights this new environment in her work, *Alone Together*. Turkle articulates the oxymoron of being isolated yet thinly connected to a large group of people:

> Technology is seductive when what it offers meets our human vulnerabilities. And as it turns out, we are very vulnerable indeed. We are lonely but fearful of intimacy. Digital connections and the sociable robot may offer the illusion of companionship without the demands of friendship. Our networked life allows us to hide from each other, even as we are tethered to each other. We'd rather text than talk. (Turkle, 2011)

To some, this is a strange concept, but one that should cause us all to pause and consider our online and offline relationships. We have the ability to connect with the world like never before, but are we really making meaningful connections?

And while technology will continue to integrate into societies and classrooms around the globe, how do we, as educators, build a classroom community comprised of meaningful relationships that can coexist with a device? How do we build a classroom community among the machines?

The answer lies in how the teacher decides to embrace new technologies without allowing them to fill in for, or take the place of, personal relationships. While this may seem challenging in today's connected classroom, being a flexible teacher is key to building a strong community. It requires balance and patience not to rush into technology just because it's available. It prompts teachers to consider how the physical space can be used as a vehicle for building a community. Ultimately, creating a classroom community demands that the teacher facilitate this process.

To start, many may think the obvious choice for building a community is a robust learning management system (LMS). While an LMS is a great tool for creating efficient workflows and organizing a classroom, it really builds a wall between the student and teacher. What's more, diving straight into an LMS produces an assembly line feeling in your classroom. Most students and teachers I talk to feel that it's a burden to read through a discussion thread and respond. Similarly, these same students and teachers also express a sense of being alone even though they are connected. The relationships are thin and practically nonexistent, yet the feeling of connectedness is present. If you've ever taken an online or virtual course, you can probably relate to these sentiments. But, how many of you remember classmates or colleagues you took an online course with? I'd venture to say those personalities are lost.

Understanding what the qualities of a strong community are beyond the technology is where all teachers should begin. The technology will come and eventually foster established relationships. These offline skill sets are extremely important to address at the elementary level. Students thrust into digital spaces too quickly may not ever come back, nor will they know a world outside of these digital spaces. Their sense of community and interaction will be diluted and, at times, seem artificial. Students, especially young students, should know what it means to have a meaningful offline relationship or friend before they have an online friend. Discerning between a best friend who lives down the street and 4,000 "friends" who live online is a difficult concept to grasp at a young and even older age. Therefore, teachers should help make this distinction early so that students can understand and successfully function as a citizen in both digital and nondigital communities.

Offline community building can be introduced in a variety of ways. I am going to give you a few to start.

1. DISCUSSION THREAD

This lesson or icebreaker is one of my favorite ways of introducing a variety of online, social media skill sets without any technology present. The setup consists of four or five tables, and each table contains a large piece of easel paper and several markers. Before your students arrive to class, draw a circle in the middle of each piece of easel paper and in the center of that circle put a word or phrase. This word or phrase can be anything you want and should be something that will spark a conversation or debate. When the students arrive, prompt them to hover around a table and remain silent. The objective is to have a conversation without saying a word. The second rule is that students must keep the conversation on paper alive. Each student will draw a line from the original circle with the word or phrase in it and add his or her thoughts. They can also add to another student's circle and continue the conversation (much like an online discussion board, blog comments, or a Facebook wall). Give each group 3 to 5 minutes to compose their thoughts and respond to others. Then students rotate to the next table. They review what the previous group posted and add to it. Students will rotate in this manner until they return to their original table. Have one student from each group hang their easel paper on the wall and allow time for the students to collectively review the different conversation threads. See Figure 3.1.

2. PERSONAL MAKERSPACE

Before your students arrive to class, place colored pipe cleaners on all of the desks. When students arrive, tell them to take their seats and create something. Again, the most important rule is silence. After about 5 minutes, pair students up randomly and have each student explain their creation. Then, have students connect in fours. Students will share each other's creations and discuss the process.

FIGURE 3.1 Developing a Conversation Thread Offline

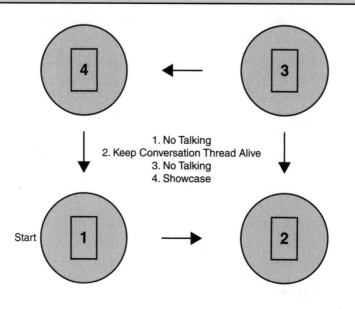

1. No Talking
2. Keep Conversation Thread Alive
3. No Talking
4. Showcase

3. POST ON MY WALL

This idea is derived from John Spencer's "Living Facebook Project."[3] During this project, John abstained from Facebook for 40 days and lived out his Facebook experience. I consolidated this project with my digital literacy class last year, but only held them to five days of no Facebook. Have students write something about themselves on your physical wall (dry-erase board). Have students respond to each other's comments as they would on a Facebook wall. Much like the discussion thread posters, have students walk around and observe and respond when they want on each other's comments.

These are only a few examples of how you can begin building classroom community among the machines. The model I am about to share employs a collaborative paradigm; however, the skill sets focus on each student learning individually to contribute to the greater goal. This lesson was designed after I made a trip to Google Offices in Cambridge, MA. My experience there opened up my eyes to how classroom space and time could be leveraged with the technology and infrastructure in place.

The objective was a challenge as opposed to learning a specific skill set.

This project did not click into motion right from the beginning. In fact, students were not really sure how to engage with a single objective and work together for a common goal. Plus, the subversive lesson in all this was that they would need each other in order to complete the challenge and inevitably get a good grade.

The other piece of this that was unorthodox was that I did not provide a specific rubric for grading. I didn't want students working toward a grade, but rather, working toward a common goal. Life is about challenges and adapting to and solving them in the most efficient and economical means possible. Therefore, this type of assignment does not require a product to demonstrate the goal. It requires students to think, question, analyze, debate, and explore the most efficient, creative solution with the resources available to them. This is how our global economy functions, and the employees with these skill sets are the ones many companies want to hire (Fischer, 2014).

Building meaningful, offline relationships is essential to engaging in digital spaces. Students must understand that a friend is not simply a button you click to accept and that a conversation is not always typed into a small box. Technology can do great things for our lives and bring us all closer together; however, it shouldn't isolate us from personal relationships.

EDUCATING THE COMMUNITY

Outside of the classroom there is a trend happening that is making many parents uneasy. This fear is the pace at which change is happening, not only with technology but the digital spaces that students dwell in on a daily basis. In the past five years, social media applications have created a new set of problems and issues for parents and guardians. Similarly, schools are facing the same issues in defining policy to enforce a set of social media acceptable use policies. Rest assured, these policies, though taking on a new medium, are policies both schools and homes have had in place for generations.

Many schools have acceptable use policies in place to support and govern the technology use around the district. These policies are legal documents that both students and parents have to sign off on before any technology can be used. Some schools create long documents explaining every detail of technology use and protocols in the building, while others simply adapt their student handbook to a digital world. Both options have merit, but again, I come back to trust and not overthinking these issues.

Eric Sheninger, principal at New Milford High School, in New Milford, NJ, has a very simplified approach to this. At New Milford High School students can bring their own devices to school and if they can't get a device, the school will support that student with a device. Their AUP greets every student when they log on to the wireless network in the building. Students hit "Accept" and they are riding the web. It's as simple as that.

The same goes for bullying. Bullying existed before the rise of digital, social spaces. The difference is in the control and reach of the message in a digital world. As early as kindergarten, students should learn about respect and how respect should not have boundaries, whether you are online or offline.

Objective:

Develop a comprehensive website for maintaining your digital identity and understanding your web privacy. Your target audience should be high school students.

Expectations:

Each student cohort is responsible for the following tasks listed in their team descriptions. Each student will receive an individual grade on this project.

Research and cover the issues below in the context of digital health and wellness. Topics can include, but are not limited to:

- maintaining digital identity,
- privacy on the web,
- cyberbullying,
- digital citizenship,
- consequences of social media misuse,
- digital access in schools (K-12), and
- social media in schools.

Teams:
Research and development

This team will be responsible for gathering information for the project. They will find resources for the website, create surveys for qualitative data collection, and put together the content for the production team. This team will have to work in conjunction with the production team and the social media and bloggers team. The R&D team will not only gather resources for others to use and cite in their work, but they will have to create thorough surveys to collect data. Finally, this team will have to create the citations for all work added to the website. Think of the R&D team as the brain of this project.

Social media and bloggers

This team will be responsible for showcasing our website. They will post blog posts that cover one of the above topics. Create media outlets for our site through Twitter, Instagram, Facebook, and so on, and build a network of followers online to discuss digital citizenship talks. This could be in the form of a Google+ hangout discussion on digital health and wellness subjects. This team is constantly moving and shaking, trying to stay ahead of the curve and keep the information current and fresh.

Production

This team will work in conjunction with the research and development team to take their research and turn it into media. They will be in charge of creating storyboards, creating scripts, filming videos, conducting interviews, and editing final products. In short, this team will do all of the media that is created. This team will not all be working on one video, but several productions within the team. It is imperative for this team to collaborate closely with the research team.

Design team

This team will be responsible for designing the layout for all of the information that we post on our site. Members of this team should have an understanding of web design and Google sites. However, even if a student has only a basic understanding of Google sites, they should still sign up for this group. This group will work in conjunction with all teams. Also, this team should be aware of what content is being created and where it would work best on the website. Finally, this team will have to be organized and use various web tools to collect data and organize it on the website.

Expectations per individual:

Each student will share a Google doc with me. This doc will be a daily log of what the student accomplishes in class. This doc will be graded and will be a major part of the student's class participation grade and overall grade. Students can do this on a Google doc or a Google spreadsheet. It should include, but is not limited to

- brainstorming ideas,
- tasks completed,
- questions raised, and
- timeline for student's work.

Grading notes . . .

Students will be graded on their interaction and engagement with their team/group. I suggest that each team, once assembled, shares a Google doc with me, and the other members should post daily progress and any information they gather. This documentation will be the bulk of the student's grade. The end result will speak for itself. I am more interested in the process, students' interaction with each other each day in class, and how students accomplish a task as a team.

25% Creativity

- Product is unique and engaging.
- Product's design is intuitive.
- Creative risks were taken to produce this product.

25% Collaboration

- Team organized daily and effectively.
- Team communicated daily and beyond the classroom.
- There is evidence of consistent communication channels.

25% Design

- Product shows evidence of creativity, uniqueness, and innovative thinking.
- Design is intuitive.
- Product is clean and error-free.

25% Spelling and Mechanics

- There are no errors in spelling or grammar.
- Presentation or demonstration is thorough and engaging.
- Planning notes and timeline are organized and clear.

The key to technology integration, at any level, is transparency with the greater school community. Technology is not a school conversation, but a community conversation. If you're integrating without educating, you've got it wrong. At both Burlington Public Schools and Groton-Dunstable Regional School District, the administration along with the tech team provided information sessions and conversations leading up to both respective technology initiatives. At Burlington we coordinated a 1:1 committee comprised of parents, students, administration, tech team members, teachers, and others. The purpose was to get collective input around a common goal: launch 1,000 iPads in the high school. These conversations happened once a month and provided consistent feedback and suggestions for our initiatives. Regardless of your model, effective integration begins and ends with a healthy balance and pace.

There is an important scene in the movie *Hoosiers* during the team's first practice. The coach, played by Gene Hackman, walks into the gym and gathers the team together. He tells his team that practice is going to be different than what they are used to. The montage that follows highlights fundamental basketball. The boys are engaged in agility drills, ball handling drills, and a variety of defensive drills. Throughout the montage you hear players asking when they are going to shoot and scrimmage. Hackman replies, "There's more to the game than shooting! There's fundamentals and defense."

This clip is the perfect segue into incorporating technology devices—iPods, iPhones, iPads, laptops, and so on—into your classroom. Before students can, to use a basketball phrase, take a shot, they must understand the fundamentals. They need to know proper footwork, stamina, and posture before they even pick up a basketball. The same principles apply to digital health and wellness and the pace at which we integrate technology.

While students and teachers alike are anxious to integrate new learning tools into the classroom, we must err on the side of caution. It is our responsibility to empower our students by giving them the fundamental lessons in digital citizenship.

Like basketball, students must enter the world of social media and digital media with a good defense. They must understand the repercussions of irresponsibly using social and digital media and what effects it may have on their future. Give students time to use the device, but make sure they understand that the device is an outlet to many new avenues.

When you are presenting social media and digital responsibility, don't lecture your students on why it is bad to post inappropriate pictures on Facebook, but have them search for examples. Allow the students to not only find examples of inappropriate use, but also allow them to teach each other. Even though they have a Facebook account, do they really understand all that comes with Facebook?

Do they understand their privacy rights on Facebook and other social media sites? Did they read the fine print?

The best offense always begins with a solid defense. This is true in sports and is directly applicable to responsible use of classroom technology and social media. While we want our students to get out there and use new and emerging technologies, we need to give them the fundamentals to play the best defense. We also want students to feel empowered when exploring digital spaces and seeking out information online. Limit restrictions and create a culture of empowered digital citizens. Brief students on the consequences of inappropriate use, but encourage them to connect, share, and discover online.

Ultimately, we want to lead by being transparent with parents and reassuring the community that the school is putting forth a best effort to not only educate students on digital citizenship, but empowering them to use it effectively. Simply removing the social network or the device is not the best way to educate our students on new and emerging technologies.

The point of this chapter is to understand that technology skill sets need to be transferable from offline to online and that you can teach these skill sets without any device in the room. Engage students in the lessons I mentioned and pace the transition from the offline world to the digital world. Think about how we all learned to drive a car. Most of us had to take a driver's education course that was mostly something we read or learned in a class. The test drive came later. And this is how we must approach technology integration. It's not healthy practice to sign a kid up for a blog before he or she has a grasp on the language and grammar. Ultimately, we must pace the integration and encourage our students to make responsible choices both online and offline.

ENDNOTES

1. http://pineglen.info/2014/03/pine-glen-digital-citizenship-featured-on-bcat/
2. http://bhsdigitallit.com/
3. http://livingfacebook.wordpress.com/

4

Remixing Professional Development

- **Supporting the technology initiative**
- **Integrating the Edcamp model**
- **Extending professional development**

One of the most frequently asked questions about shifting a school district to a shared culture of learning that is transparent and engaging lies in the category of professional development (PD). For years, professional development has been a constant in the field of education; however, its design has needed work. The real hypocrisy with professional development is that we are constantly seeking ways to differentiate our instruction, but we have never done so with professional development. In a sense, professional development, for the most part, has been a passive experience for teachers and something they have to do, as opposed to wanting to do.

However, change has and is happening in the category of professional development. In May 2010, Edcamp Philly[1] disrupted the traditional model of professional development and launched a global movement. An Edcamp is organic, free, user-driven professional development that allows everyone in attendance a voice. There is no schedule, no keynote, and no vendors. Simply, an Edcamp is about learning and doing, not just sitting and checking boxes.

Schedule PD That Allows Time to Explore and Share

If your EdTech professional development resembles a TED Talk, you might want to reconsider the method of delivery. This is not to say that lecture is an ineffective means of delivering content, but EdTech PD should include time to explore. It should be hands on, and groups or teams should have time to share their learning.

In working with schools, I've suggested that districts employ the Edcamp model for remixing their professional development. This model allows everyone to participate, share, and be heard. Teachers walk away from this kind of PD ready to integrate what they've learned in the classroom. Also, administrators should model personal learning networks and leverage a wide range of social media for on-demand learning opportunities.

Integrating the Edcamp Format

The Edcamp model of professional develop just makes sense. Some would argue that there is not enough research to validate Edcamp's credibility; however, sometimes common sense is the best research model.

When I helped launch the 1:1 iPad rollout in Burlington Public Schools in 2011, one of the biggest questions floating in the air was "How are we going to prep every teacher and student on the iPad?" Time was not on our side. Our rollout started with teachers. Teachers received their iPad in June at the end of school. They were given a brief overview of the device and a few apps to check out over the summer. And that was phase one. Nothing more. Sometimes we tend to overthink and overteach when it comes to professional development and even classroom practice. In many scenarios, letting someone try, fail, try again, get frustrated, and learn is the best practice. This is not to say we were negligent with training our staff, but rather we trusted them as professionals to adjust to the device and use the support of the tech team as a resource.

The next phase we provided was "Edcamp Tuesdays" throughout the summer. In short, every Tuesday after the Fourth of July, the Burlington EdTech team would be on hand at the high school library from 8 a.m. to noon to facilitate morning sessions on a variety of subjects. We didn't construct a schedule, but simply served as a presence and support for teachers who wanted to visit, share, and learn more about the device both they and the students would be using on a daily basis.

Initially, the Tuesday Edcamps were attended lightly, but it picked up, with many teachers arriving along with teachers and administrators from other area school districts. The meetings were casual and engaging. Some attendees stepped up and led short demos or presentations on applications they had discovered or used in a lesson. However, the focus was not on who could share the most apps, but rather, "How are we going to leverage this device in the classroom?"

As the summer passed and the calendar inched closer to the first day of school, Dennis Villano, director of Instructional Technology at Burlington Public Schools, and I began preparations for an unprecedented event in late August. That event was called BPScon. As a district, we decided to front load our professional development days and create a conference-like atmosphere for three consecutive days the week before school started. The event started on a Monday and would wrap up on a Wednesday. On Thursday teachers would have time to prep classrooms and hold team meetings. Friday was a day off before the Labor Day weekend.

BPScon[2] was constructed like a conference, and we had four scheduled time slots each day and provided five or six options per time slot. In some scenarios, we had to schedule in mandatory events. This meant that the second-grade teachers had to schedule the first session Monday to learn about standards-based report cards. So, while there was freedom and flexibility built into the schedule, we had to make sure all mandatory meetings were met.

For scheduling, we used an app called SCHED.org, which allowed teachers to build their own schedule throughout the three days. We also included paper sign-in sheets for each session so teachers could track PD hours.

The presenters were all colleagues. We did not hire any outside speakers, but teachers learned from teachers (and in some cases students). Most of the sessions were conducted in a standard presentation-style format, but we did include some hands-on workshops that included iPads. During the first year a lot of the sessions revolved around the iPad, Google Apps for Education, and X2 (our Student Information System).[3] While some may argue that these topics made it more about the devices and apps than the teaching and learning, it was necessary to take care of basics of the technology so that teachers could leverage the devices effectively. At some point, it does need to be about the technology. In years two and three sessions of BPScon, we shifted toward a more integrated model where we were no longer just showcasing apps, but evidence of classroom use, lessons, and ideas.

Overall, the three days of BPScon were a large success. Teachers enjoyed the opportunity for choice and felt that they didn't have to sit in an auditorium for an entire day and passively learn by being talked at by speakers. We even included health and wellness sessions in the form of yoga, outside walks, and origami. Plus, we had our Burlington High School student help desk on hand to run an on-site Genius Bar. The experience was a great one for our students, and the feedback from staff was glowing. Basically, anytime throughout the day staff could stop by the "EdTech Commons."

Keeping the Momentum

While we had many successes with our summer professional development and deployments, the real challenge arises when students enter the building on day one. As an administrator, how do you keep that momentum going throughout the year? As an educator, how do you keep the momentum and excitement going throughout the year in your respective classroom? As a student, how do you find time among academics and extracurricular activities to leverage a device that you have now been entrusted with?

These questions, and more, arise once you have your deployment off the ground and running. This is where your administration and tech team need to be on the same page as you move forward and try to find ways to sustain momentum around education technology initiatives.

Below, in Figure 4.1, is a flowchart I developed to conceptualize how professional development is changing or how professional development should change. It should include plenty of time for conversation, tinkering, and exploration and discovery. Professional development of this nature should have an end goal and should be something that teachers can practically integrate within a comfortable timeframe. If you're providing top-down, mandated professional development that is a passive experience, you might want to reevaluate the effectiveness of this model.

In short, this chart highlights the importance of district and school professional development. There must be time for all of the above circles to connect, share, and learn together—and yield a product or example that can be shared and archived for the district to use in future professional development presentations, or simply as a

FIGURE 4.1 Professional Development 2.0

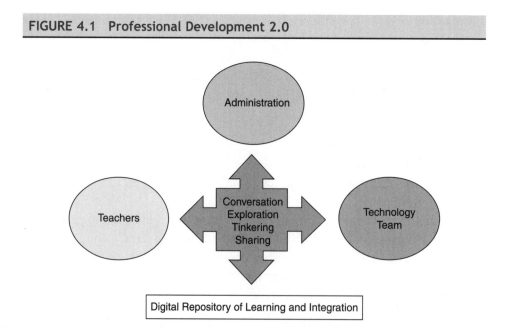

resource. Regardless of how you interpret the above model, professional development should be democratic and led by the voice of the teacher.

As a tech team, we created several forums throughout the school year for both teachers and parents to get information on technology initiatives that were happening and proposed for future consideration. Every Tuesday the Burlington EdTech team held weekly "How Do I Do That?"[4] sessions at a different school each week. Initially, these sessions offered teachers a place to come after hours and get assistance with technology and ask questions. Some teachers wanted to set up a blog while some just wanted to learn how to efficiently organize Gmail. In short, we borrowed Apple's model of customer support and integrated it directly into our district.

The same event took place during several simultaneous technology deployments at Groton-Dunstable Regional School District. I integrated the Genius Bar[5] concept every Thursday and rotated different schools each week. Initially, we had an open forum for questions and support. After the first few sessions the team decided to provide focused sessions each week. At first, the tech team members ran these sessions. We eventually had teachers and administrators asking if they could present as well. This was a great transition for everyone and helped expand the collective voice and mission of tech integration.

In addition to our Thursday Genius Bar, we created EdTech "Flashmobs" at a different school each week. We did not integrate a song or dance, but organized as many members of the tech team as possible on one day, and spread ourselves throughout that school. We visited classrooms, held drop-in sessions for teachers and students, and simply presented ourselves for any kind of help needed throughout any given day. In addition, this gave the tech team a good gauge on what schools needed in regard to tech and helped address any outstanding issues.

The Groton-Dunstable tech team also held monthly Community Tech Nights. The purpose of these monthly sessions was to educate the community and parents on what technology students have access to, as well as trending topics around parenting in the digital age. Initially, we focused our sessions on what students were using. For example, we launched several new initiatives at the beginning of the 2013–2014 school year. One of the biggest transitions was to Google Apps for Education. This suite of apps was launched to our entire staff and student populations. For the first time in our district, students had e-mail accounts K–12. The first conversation session we had with parents focused on what students had access to and what they could do with their new accounts. Sessions that followed were:

- *Social Media and Your Student*

- *Understanding Privacy Settings*

- *iPads for Parents*

- *Connecting with Your Child*

During our first year of 1:1 iPad, we used our time wisely throughout the district. For our districtwide professional development days at the high school, we flipped a few days into Edcamp-like models of sharing and learning. The plan is simple: Teachers gathered initially by department and discussed ways in which they were using the iPad in their classes and in their disciplines. Everyone shared and then one or several representatives demonstrated how they were using the iPad in their content area in front of the entire faculty. This was not an app-centric sharing moment; rather, teachers shared with teachers how they were leveraging the device in order to impact teaching and learning. Each demonstration was recorded and archived for follow-up from staff.

And this is just one scenario that worked for us at Burlington. Another way to engage staff and broaden perspective would incorporate a similar model, but we would change it up just a little. The second scenario works similar to the first, except instead of staying in department cohorts, departments rotate on a scheduled cycle so that they eventually connect with each department and are privy to more sharing opportunities across the content areas.

Below are examples that were shared from one of our professional development sessions where we discussed best practices with the iPad.

1) French IV by Madame Price (@TwinsBless on Twitter)

We are in the middle of reading a Canadian detective novel, *L'Affaire Québécoise*. It has 20 chapters. I had each student select a scene from a favorite chapter and make a video. They sent in the text via the writing application VidEditor,[6] which is a free app. When the students finished with their video, they instantly uploaded it to our class YouTube account.

FRENCH IV

L'Affaire Québécoise / un projet de video avec VidEditor Free App

RESPONSIBILITIES

1. Vous allez travailler en groupe de trois élèves.
2. Vous choisirez un thème.
3. Il faut soumettre UN (1) video par groupe.
4. Vous devez soumettre aussi le texte attaché dans un App pour écrire pour votre video.
5. Il est important d'avoir la musique au fond de votre video.
6. Il est nécessaire de parler avec un bon accent. Vous êtes acteurs / actrices à une émission de programme à la télé en France.

2) French V by Madame Price

My French V students just finished reading the classic *Le Petit Prince*. We have the English version in our iBooks and the French version on a PDF that we accessed through

Notability.[7] This rich novel is filled with many philosophical themes. I had the students select just 10 of their most memorable themes and illustrate them with videos. In addition to describing in the target language why they selected these themes, they also had to illustrate how these themes related to their own lives. They, too, sent in their text on a familiar Notability. As was evident while viewing these videos, there was substantial student-directed activity, engagement in the learning process, and a familiarity with technology that, in my estimation, enhances learning.

FRENCH V

LPP / PROJECT FINAL POUR: *Le Petit Prince*

Vous allez utiliser VidEditor Free et un autre App pour écrire. (Notability)

RESPONSIBILITIES

1. Choisissez dix (10) thèmes en *Le Petit Prince.*
2. Ecrivez les dix thèmes SUR UN APP POUR ECRIRE.
3. Illustrez-les avec des vrais objets. N'UTILISEZ PAS DE PHOTOS OU D'IMAGES DE GOOGLE, PAS DE CLIP ART, ETC. IL FAUT UTILISER VidEditor Free de PRENDRE DES VRAIS PHOTOS!!!
   a. LA PARTIE ORALE: Parlez de l'importance de cet objet dans le roman et du thème.
   b. Parlez-moi de l'importance de l'importance de ce thème en votre vie.
4. LA PARTIE ECRITE: Ecrivez ce dont vous avez parlé dans un App pour écrire.
5. Soumettez votre video à YouTube
6. Envoyez vos phrases (SmartNote, Noterize, Paper Port Notes, etc.) àprice@bpsk12.org.

NE COPIEZ PAS DU ROMAN NI UTILISEZ DE TRADUCTEUR!! ECRIVEZ VOS PROPRES PHRASES!!!

STUDENT WORK VIDEO LINKS[8]

3) Calculus by Brighid Boyle

Recently, Ms. Boyle's calculus students were given an end-of-semester project that prompted them to teach a calculus lesson through the medium of a music video. The students filmed the videos on their iPads and then edited using iMovie. Each group had two weeks to create a script and storyboard, and then film, edit, and present the lesson. The results were not only engaging, but also informative. Consider it the musical version of Khan Academy. The results are displayed below. Enjoy, share, and learn!

STUDENT WORK VIDEO LINKS[9]

4) Trigonometry by Dan Calore

For this lesson, I wanted to change the way that students did standard lab reports in math. I felt that the standard lab was not teaching the students to explain and fully understand what it was they were working on. I created a lab in which the report was either a YouTube video or a video using the show-me application to describe in detail the problem they were solving and how they solved it. I tried this on the grounds that in business you often have to present a problem or solution to coworkers, and with video conferencing and e-mail output I felt this would allow the students a chance to work on their presentation skills as well.

Trig Lab 1: Using Right Triangle Trig for Real Applications

1. You are going to use right triangle trigonometry to determine either the height of an object or the speed at which an object is moving.

EXAMPLES: Determine the height of the flagpole using the length of the shadow cast and angle of elevation to the sun; or determine the speed that someone is running by finding the angle to the start location and the angle at the end of the run, and then time the runner.

Assignment: Due at the end of class on Thursday, December 8, 2011

Either create a video that shows you finding the measurements to your problem and then explaining how you solve for your missing parts; or use the show-me application to teach how to solve the problem, from getting the information to finding the final answer. The goal of the write-up is to explain your work so that anyone can duplicate it and get the same results. Answer in detail each of the following questions and discuss units used, methodology used to gather the data, trig functions used, and any assumptions that you made.

Questions to be answered:

1. What are you trying to solve for? How are you going to solve for it?
2. What are the known values, and how did you determine them?
3. What did you do to solve for the unknown values?
4. Draw an *accurate* diagram to represent the problems.
5. Conclusion

5) History by Michael Milton (@42ThinkDeep on Twitter)

What better way to make the Enlightenment come alive than to have my World History students create Blogger sites and set up a conversation on Twitter!

In our activity, students were hired by a consulting firm to bring the ideas of the Enlightenment to a modern "tech-savvy" audience. In small groups, they assumed the identities of various philosophers (Voltaire, the Baron De Montesquieu, John Locke, Thomas Hobbes, Mary Wollstonecraft, and Jean Jacques Rousseau) and wrote a blog post to reintroduce them to the world and to discuss how their ideas were incorporated into the United States of America. The posts were then shared under a common hashtag, and students, as the philosophers, began interacting with one another.

For the next step, I wanted students to extrapolate the ideas of their philosophers into other historical situations. For instance, a question for Rousseau might be, "What are your views on communism and how it worked in Russia during the reign of Stalin?" To answer this question, students not only have to research communism, specifically communism under Stalin, but they also have to figure out how Rousseau would view both. Now, I could have simply asked the questions myself, but I felt that my students would get more excited to do this research if they were answering to a larger audience. I shared this assignment with my colleagues and my personal learning network (PLN), who then shared it with their PLNs.

My students really got into the activity, particularly when they realized that they were playing for a larger audience. For 83 minutes (a long block), my students were in research and publication mode. They were engaging with those outside of the classroom, as well as with each other. I played the role of the facilitator, ensuring that all students were engaged. Overall, my students were able to form a deeper understanding of the philosophers of the Enlightenment and were introduced to both Twitter and Blogger.

6) Digital Literacy by Andy Marcinek (@AndyCinek on Twitter)

Objective: Demonstrate what you have learned throughout this class. Consider the Google Zeitgeist 2011[10] video we watched prior to break. It should work as a demonstration of what you learned as opposed to a retelling of applications and ideas you learned.

NOTE: I'm not looking for a PowerPoint presentation.

Requirements: Creatively show what you have learned from the course.
- *You may want to demonstrate how you will use these skills in the future.*
- *You may want to highlight one application or multiple applications that appeal to you.*
- *You may want to present on a specific subject such as digital health and wellness, digital identity, social media, privacy, or creative commons.*
- *You may want to create something entirely new using the applications and ideas you gleaned from this course.*
- *You may want to create a movie trailer for this course.*
- *You may want to create a documentary about this course.*
- *Or, you may want to do something completely different.*

Grading: You will be graded on your ability to clearly demonstrate to an audience your learning over the past few weeks. I will be looking for the following items in your final work:
- *Creativity*
- *Engagement*
- *Understanding*
- *Proficiency*

- *Presentation*
- *Participation (in class)*

Presentations and demonstrations will begin on January 11 and conclude on January 13.

STUDENT WORK LINK[11]

All of the above lessons are not iPad specific, nor do they teach to the technology. Instead, teachers are synthesizing the device with a rich curriculum. If we continue to halt technology integration and access in our schools, then we'll continue to restrict our students' learning. There is not one way to change or reform education, so don't limit your school to the current trend or buzzword that happens to trickle down your Twitter column or grace the front page of the latest education journal. Take a simple approach and don't overthink or overanalyze this change. It's not about a technology device; rather, it's about evolving your school culture to create dynamic learning spaces that embrace a shared culture of learning. Whatever ratio you decide to go with, and no matter what device you choose, know that you will be providing students with purposeful learning experiences that integrate relevant technologies.

EXTENDING PD OPPORTUNITIES

At Burlington, along with Dennis Villano, we created a weekly PD opportunity called, "How Do I Do That?" sessions. Initially, we held these events twice a month on a Tuesday. There was a schedule of topics and presenters as well. While these sessions were well attended and beneficial to our district, we decided to shift the model the following year because many teachers came to our sessions for support along with the topic at hand. What we found was that teachers were excited about learning more on the given subject, but they needed some time to simply connect with one of our team members.

The following year we did not schedule any sessions or topics, had the events every Tuesday of the year after school, and rotated between schools each week. This worked much better, but there were some who longed for the previous system. When I started at Groton-Dunstable Regional School District as the director of technology, one of the first items on my agenda was to integrate a similar model for ongoing optional professional development throughout the year. We did not integrate a three-day conference-like back-to-school PD, but rather we opened up a Genius Bar for the first few days of school, where teachers could drop in at designated areas at their respective schools and get any type of tech help. The team also coordinated similar sessions throughout the school year, and we offered our Genius Bar after school—every Thursday for one hour, or as long as people needed to field questions. Initially, we had an open forum for questions relating to EdTech; however, we decided to provide a focus each week as we rotated schools. So, each week we posted our schedule of sessions being offered at the upcoming Genius Bar, who was facilitating it, and a brief description. This format allowed teachers an opportunity to plan and check off times when they could attend. We also had members of our tech team available to field miscellaneous questions.

When it comes to new initiatives in a school system, time is always of the essence. At both Burlington and Groton-Dunstable, I had to find creative methods to bring in optional professional development options, while not demanding too much. In any new technology initiative, the tech team along with administration must work collaboratively to maximize the workload of rolling out any large- or small-scale initiative. Plus, there should always be a healthy balance between introducing new technology and applications and curriculum and instruction. Eventually, the two sides intersect and yield great lessons and projects, but it's essential that one not overshadow the other.

One of the best moves I helped create at both Burlington and Groton-Dunstable was student help desk courses. These courses are half-year elective courses that are designed to promote a workshop-style classroom for students who are interested in working with and learning more about technology in education.

These are only a few examples of how a school district can begin to rethink professional development. Also, this is not to say that every form of professional development or faculty meeting needs to be flipped on its head; however, there should be a healthy balance of several models throughout the year and summer months. Ultimately, these models should include several key factors:

1. Time for conversation

2. Time for hands-on exploration

3. Time for making mistakes

4. Time for sharing

5. Time to reflect

In the next chapter I will share the experience of involving students in district professional development and how they helped support our technology initiatives. For school administrators, cultivating a culture of shared learning is essential when establishing new initiatives. Whether these initiatives are related to technology or pedagogy, administrators want to offer a variety of options for learning and seek out ways to differentiate professional development. Additionally, it's essential to encourage conversations, exploration, and sharing within PD paradigms. And finally, encourage staff to take educated risks and promote classroom innovation. There's always the chance that this practice could go wrong or fall short of expectations, but consider it a learning moment. It's not a failure until you quit.

ENDNOTES

1. http://www.edcampphilly.org/
2. http://bpscon.org/
3. http://www.follettsoftware.com/school-administration-software
4. http://www.bpsedtech.org/2014/05/06/how-do-i-do-that-may-2014/
5. http://gdrsdedtech.org/2013/10/09/the-gdrsd-edtech-genius-bar/
6. https://itunes.apple.com/us/app/video-editor-for-free/id450722848?mt=8
7. https://itunes.apple.com/us/app/notability/id360593530?mt=8
8. http://youtu.be/k8LKnqolVjQ and http://youtu.be/X4QN-AM_QsY
9. http://youtu.be/mGd0bp7vOlI and http://youtu.be/hpgbPeMDMyA
10. https://www.youtube.com/watch?v=SAIEamakLoY
11. http://youtu.be/FdEXijFXfD8

The Case for a Student Help Desk

- **What is a student-run help desk?**
- **The help desk structure**
- **Authentic learning experiences**

If you ask anyone at Burlington Public Schools what was one of the best outcomes of the 1:1 iPad initiative, they'd tell you it was the student help desk. The student help desk not only provided a unique learning opportunity for students, but it also effectively supported our 1:1 initiative. Burlington Public Schools' director of technology, Bob Cunha, said this initiative would have happened with or without the help desk addition, but it made the tech team's job a lot smoother with it involved. Most importantly, Cunha could focus his time and energy on managing and maintaining a robust network, while students in the help desk took care of password resets and Wi-Fi issues.

During our first year with the help desk course we allowed any student to take the course. What we learned is that we weren't so much looking for students interested in computers, but students who were self-directed learners. This learning moment led to setting up interviews for students who elected to take the course. Students had to sign up for a time, show up with a resume, and engage in a brief interview. We asked the students a variety of questions and then had them go through a battery of tests. For example, we turned off the Wi-Fi on one of the devices and asked the student to see what the problem was. We weren't looking for the quickest fix, rather, for a student who could deconstruct a problem and know when to move on and come back to it later. We also wanted students to offer a "plan B" for issues they could not immediately resolve.

In this chapter I will share the two courses I created at Burlington High School and at Groton-Dunstable Regional High School. I will also share stories of students who took the course. These personal accounts will not only reinforce the impact of this course but also offer evidence for how technology can impact a student both academically and throughout his or her career. I'll start with the course description below:

The Student Technology Integration course is a hands-on study of technology integration in an educational context. Students will be required to assess problem sets throughout the day and define the best approach to addressing or solving the problem. In addition to solving problems for their classmates and teachers, students will be required to complete and maintain several running projects that address problems or solutions in educational technology integration. The course also asks students to have a prior understanding of Apple OS, Microsoft Windows OS, and the iPad iOS.

Welcome to BHS Help Desk. This course will examine various problems and needs throughout Burlington High School. This semester, we will not be waiting around for problems to come to us, we will be finding and addressing them. This is not to say we won't encounter problems here in the Help Desk room, but we will be more aggressive in seeking out the problems and needs of our faculty and students.

This semester we will not only be helping, but creating, curating and organizing information and content for the faculty and students. This may come in the form of a blog that you manage for a department. It may be building an iBook resource companion for one of your teachers. It may be building a set of instructional videos and books for the school to use. In short, we will have plenty of work to do throughout the course of this semester. Whatever you heard about Help Desk during season one will not surface during season two. Help Desk has changed, and in order to maintain a good grade in this class, you will need to perform. This course will elicit and require skills that are relevant to most professions.

We have also added new features to the help desk this year so that we concentrate our talent in the right areas of need.

Help Desk Opportunities for Faculty and Staff

1. Help Desk Tutorials

During the second semester, teachers can schedule time during their free periods and come down to Help Desk for a one-on-one tutorial of your choice. This can be on a specific application that you want to learn more about or just an overview of the iPad or your computer. We will match you with a Help Desk student and you will have as much time as needed during that period. You can sign up **here** for Help Desk tutorials. This feature is also open to students. If you would like your class to learn how to use an application before starting a project, we can assist with this as well.

2. Share and Connect

(This opportunity is primarily for the teachers, but you may be asked to help with organizing and teaching this platform.) I want to start highlighting the amazing work you and your students have been doing over the past semester on our bpsedtech.org[1] blog. If you have a lesson that you designed that you are proud of along with student work that came out of that project, please share a short write up of the lesson and links to any student work.

3. In Class Assistance

If you would like Help Desk students to assist with or set up equipment for a lesson you are conducting in class, you can sign up **here** for that time. This student will be scheduled to meet with you during your period for as long as you need him or her.

4. Help Desk on Twitter

If you are using Twitter, you can now access Help Desk by using the hashtag #bhshelpdesk. This will give us a method of responding to your issue immediately.

5. The BHS Resource Wiki

(This is primarily for the teachers, but you may be asked to help with organizing and teaching this platform.) I mentioned this wikispace at the beginning of the year and want to have departments take over the space and add resources to it as they populate. Once approved, you can add a page or create one for sharing resources with your entire department throughout the year. Think of it as a digital communal file cabinet. Also, as we move toward creating more ePubs, this space will be good for gleaning resources when they are needed. If you have any questions about the wiki please contact me.

Help Desk Pathways

1. Bloggers

Bloggers will be responsible for authoring and maintaining a blog for departments, teachers and Help Desk. We will be creating a comprehensive student Help Desk blog that must be updated daily. Each day there should be new content populating on the site; therefore, you will need to find and create information to post. This can come in the form of a

(Continued)

weekly podcast, interviews, original posts, reaction posts to current events regarding technology, or short documentaries that you create on specific subjects. Regardless of the subject, this site should be flourishing with new content each day.

2. Genius Bar Trainers

The Genius Bar Trainers will be responsible for deconstructing daily problems with the technology at the school. This job will require an expertise in a variety of applications or the willingness to learn new applications. Also, this path of the course will require competency in Apple iLife and iWork programs (iPhoto, iMovie, Pages, Numbers, etc.). Participants will be giving one-on-one tutorials to teachers, staff and students. You may be required to enter a classroom and present an overview of an application before the teacher uses it with his or her class. When you are not training, you will be putting together tutorial videos, scripts and iBooks.

3. App Developer Course

The App Developer Course will be the most challenging section of the course, but potentially the most rewarding. Participants will be taking the Stanford University iPad and iPhone App Developer Course via their iPad and iTunes U. This course will be very challenging and time consuming. While you should already have an understanding of some programming, it is not required.

4. iBooks Authors

This pathway will help teachers, administration and staff with creating ePubs or iBooks. You should have an understanding of Apple Pages and the new iBooks Author application. The majority of the time you will be migrating content from either analog or digital form into these two applications. A lot of the time will be spent on formatting and adding images, video and audio clips to the publication. Also, if you are unfamiliar with these applications but possess a willingness to learn them, please sign up for this pathway.

5. Choose Your Own Adventure

You also have the opportunity to propose a pathway for second semester. In your proposal you must define your goals, objectives, resources needed, and the hurdles you may encounter along the way. I would also like you to detail the impact you expect your pathway to have on Burlington High School.

Tasks and Assignments

1. Help Desk Journal

Regardless of the course path you choose, you will document your productivity each day via a Google Doc journal. At the end of each class or each night, you will post your progress for the day. Note that I will view the timestamp for each daily post, so this is not something you should cram together Friday afternoon. Also, this is not simply busy work, but a running dialogue of your Help Desk progress. On occasion, I will not be in class and helping with a problem, so you must maintain productivity and transparency.

Each post should include what you accomplished for the day, who you helped or what you learned. Depending on which path you take and what you accomplish for the day, your post may come in the form of a link, video or brief blurb. It could also come in the form of a problem you are having and your attempt to reconcile that problem. Also, there may be a point in the course where you feel that you have to do some work or study quickly for a test. This is fine on occasion, but do not turn Help Desk into a study hall. If you abuse this opportunity, your grade will suffer.

2. Help Desk Meetings
We will conduct Monday and Friday meetings to check in on how things are going. Most of the time you will be working independently throughout this course, so this will be our opportunity to check in with each other and address any questions.

Source: Groton-Dunstable Regional School District

STUDENT HELP DESK RESULTS

There is no doubt that the student technology integration course (Help Desk) at Burlington was a glowing success, both with students and our school community. I had the opportunity to work with several students throughout my two years overseeing this course, and I have continued to stay in touch with the course through the new Help Desk teacher. She has carried on this course and made great strides in adapting it and making it her own.

Over the past two years, Burlington High School Help Desk students spoke and presented at MassCUE (Computer Using Educators), which is held at Gillette Stadium in Foxboro, MA. In both instances, the students shined and not only owned their learning, but they were able to eloquently convey how this course had impacted their learning and career paths.

For Help Desk students, this course was not just a computer course or technology course, but a course in life. Students were asked daily to solve problems both individually and collaboratively. Students had to interact on a professional level with their peers, their teachers, and former teachers. Plus, administration regularly called on students to assist with technology and digital projects throughout the year. The Help Desk students designed and maintained blogs for several departments at the high school, as well as helped principals and assistant principals begin to blog and create a digital space. Students worked alongside us at professional development events such as BPScon and after-school Genius Bars.

In short, the benefits of this course were seen through the actions and accomplishments of the students. This course did not have exams or quizzes; rather, every day was an exam, a quiz in what each student could do when faced with a real problem. And in education, this is where we must lead our students. For too long, creative, high-stakes testing has overshadowed inquiry-driven learning. Courses like Help Desk are just the beginning in what can be a creative approach to teaching and learning. The technology simply supports these new paradigms for classroom and instructional design.

AUTHENTIC LEARNING PROJECTS

STUDENTS ORGANIZE AND HOST AN EDCAMP

One of the elements I enjoy most about being a teacher is the element of surprise. I'm referring to that moment when a student or group of students really amazes you. You mentor these students, give them your best as a teacher day in and day out without any required thanks, and occasionally this student or group of students unintentionally returns the favor in the form of intrinsic motivation. They're driven because they find purpose in what they are learning or doing. This couldn't be more evident than with my Help Desk students who organized EdCampxEDU.[2]

This was the first, to my knowledge, Edcamp designed, organized, and carried out entirely by students. While I have been an advisor to these students, I have remained on the periphery of this project. Initially, I met with students who were interested in organizing this event and gave them the run-down on what the format was and how an Edcamp functioned. Having organized three NTCamps (an Edcamp format for new teachers) and created and run Edcamp Tuesdays at Burlington High School along with Dennis Villano,[3] I knew what it took to make an Edcamp work. It's a daunting task for any team of organizers.

The EdCampxEDU organizers stepped up to the challenge. During this project I observed the team starting to receive prizes from various vendors to give out on June 1, I watched as they planned the opening address, and saw them prep the final details of planning. Oh, and when the organization team is not planning EdCampxEDU, they are at track or baseball practice, attending a full schedule of classes, or getting ready for work at their part-time jobs. Some even managed to fit in prom.

This experience will impact them more than any SAT exam, AP test, or MCAS test. This experience provides students with the opportunity to elicit skill sets and apply them to a purposeful scenario. It's project-based and challenge-based learning at its best. It meets the needs of many Common Core standards and is something that will stand out on any college application or resume. This team will get to say:

"I designed, organized, and carried out an education conference."

"I managed a budget and networked with vendors."

"I used social media for advertising and web 2.0 tools for marketing and promotion."

I am proud of these students. And I know that this type of project gave them a wealth of new skill sets and exposed them to many new challenges and opportunities that they might not have otherwise had.

GILAD'S STORY

I had one of those conversations recently that I won't forget. But first, let me provide some context to this story. While I was teaching the Help Desk course last fall at Burlington High School, I had a student ask his guidance counselor if he could work on one of the iMac machines that had XCODE installed on it during 5th period every Thursday. I agreed and took on Gilad as an independent study.

Every Thursday Gilad quietly entered the help desk room and opened XCODE. Our interaction was limited, but over his shoulder I could see he was doing work far beyond my knowledge base. Gilad entered the same way every Thursday for four months. Around January, he asked me if we had a developer account with Apple. We did. I set him up with Bob Cunha (Burlington director of technology), who got him set up, his device registered, and explained the process of app submission.

In a matter of a few months, Gilad had taken time out of his study hall and developed a voice recording and submission application that will eventually be used by the Burlington High School Guidance Department for setting up appointments with students.

A few months later, Gilad approached me during lunch and asked if I knew of any programming opportunities or internships for the summer. I said I would check back with him and started seeking out my network. I contacted two friends at Google in Cambridge first. Unfortunately, they did not have anything at the time. Plus, most of their deadlines had already past. I continued to search until I remembered my brief consulting work I did with MobileAware[4] in early 2012. I contacted my friend, MobileAware CEO Armin Gebauer, to see if he had any openings for internships. He mentioned that they had just created an iOS development team. I connected Gebauer with Gilad, and they eventually set up an interview. Gilad soon accepted the internship and had been working there for a few weeks when I wrote a blog on the topic; below is an excerpt.

Yesterday, I decided to check in with Gilad to see how he was doing. Here is the transcript of our brief conversation:

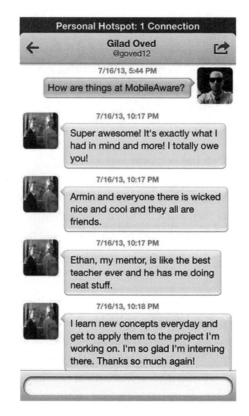

Source: Gilad Oved

And this is why yesterday was a good day for me. I was able to establish a connection for a student and help him find a learning environment that not only challenges him, but connects him with professionals who can mentor and inspire him. And that, I feel, is part of being a good teacher and connected educator.

I'm not writing this post to boast. I simply phoned up a connection and made a match. The piece of this that caused me to pause and reflect is how the connection was made. In many circles I hear the first step to being a connected educator is Twitter. It's imperative that we, as educators, sign up for Twitter and dive head first into an oncoming wave.

Respectfully, I have to disagree with this sentiment (which is a generalization for the most part). While Twitter has its merits, it will never match personal connections.

I connected with Armin by accident. I just happened to sit next to him and his wife one night out for dinner. Being two extroverts, Armin and I began discussing our work and it led to me getting hired as a consultant with MobileAware. When my tenure ended at MobileAware, I continued to connect with Armin. I connected with Gilad through his guidance counselor. And finally I connected Armin with Gilad.

I'm not trying to argue the merits of Twitter but simply offer a different path for new teachers looking to test the waters of social media. There are days when I can't quite grasp the credibility of Twitter voices: the blind re-tweeting, the pseudo celebrity aura, the echo chamber, the hierarchy, the "let's change the etymology of the word 'cheating'" (and every other word in order to show a progressive, "disruptor I am" persona). It's deafening. And quite frankly, if I were mentoring a new teacher, I'd tell them to hold off on Twitter.

Consider making personal, in person connections in lieu of Twitter. And, when you're ready, embrace Twitter but develop a way to filter your stream and vet your following for credibility. Spend a lot of time listening, processing, and actually reading what's being shared. And finally, don't get caught up in the noise. I encourage Twitter use among educators, but balk at the idea of it being necessary for all new and current teachers. It's simply a tool. A tool that I've embraced criticized and used to share many of these posts.

Before we rush our new teachers or students into the world of Twitter, let's take a moment to forge a personal, meaningful connection with them. Establish credibility and take time to listen and engage. In doing so you may just help find that student or teacher find their passion.

RYAN'S STORY

At Groton-Dunstable Regional School District, I encountered a similar burst of intrinsic motivation that left me, well, gobsmacked at what a student accomplished. I'll try and capture this story concisely.

On July 1, 2013, I started my tenure as the director of technology for Groton-Dunstable Regional School District. My first job was to provide advocacy and support for technology throughout our district. Groton-Dunstable is a district that consists of a wonderful, supportive community, progressive, dedicated educators and administration, and students who are bright and kind. Up until my arrival, technology was an afterthought. This is not to say that the tech team was not working hard or dedicated, but simply, there was no voice or leadership for technology in the district.

My first two initiatives included upgrading the network infrastructure districtwide and transitioning our staff from a first-class e-mail system to a Google Apps for Education environment that would include accounts for both teachers and students. I also purchased 600 Chromebooks for students to use across five schools. And this is where the story begins.

We were in the process of organizing 600 Chromebooks into groups and carts for each school to use. Plus, I wanted to match the serial numbers on each device with a cart. When you enroll Chromebooks, they enroll but are not grouped. (**NOTE:** *There may be a way of automatically enrolling into specific groups, but I had some inconsistencies with auto-enroll.*) So the solution was to group the Chromebooks into 25, enroll them, and then plug them into carts while documenting the serial numbers. A cumbersome process, nonetheless.

When I arrived at Groton-Dunstable Regional High School later that week, I was greeted by some of the Tech Task Force students. The Tech Task Force takes the help desk model I created at Burlington High School and presents it with a different name and schedule.

I walked in and noticed Ryan scanning the back of the Chromebooks. To me, it looked as if he was taking a picture of each device's serial number and bar code. He wasn't. He said

> I actually created a script with Python that uses an Android API for a bar code scanner that will scan the device's bar code and push it directly to a CSV file.[5]

Of course you did.

He did this on his own, without any demand from us. This was not homework, the state or federal government will not test him on it, and he did not receive a rubric or a grade. Ryan simply saw a problem and developed an efficient solution using a skill set that in many schools is not being taught. And I'm not referring to computer science, but simply time to create, develop, and explore beyond a common curriculum. Ryan saved our tech team a few days' worth of work and impressed me beyond anything I expected to see that Friday morning.

Ryan is not common and does not fit into the Common Core curriculum. Ryan has raced beyond what our federal government deems "the top." Most ETS tests are beneath Ryan. And, while I understand that not all students are like Ryan and the moment I witnessed was very unique, it doesn't create an excuse for rethinking and redesigning our education system. America needs a system that fosters creativity, exploration and discovery, mistakes, and innovation. That's a system that we owe our students.

Again, these courses and stories were not possible because we were lucky enough to have 1,000 iPads at the school or a half a million dollar technology grant, but simply administration and educators who were willing to push forward with and support progressive teaching opportunities. That's it. The technology is only a fraction of this puzzle and can never replace good teaching.

Finally, I want to share an experience that involved students I taught at Burlington High School. This next story was one that was never fully realized, but the experience was amazing for the students who were a part of it.

Burlington High School students had the opportunity to visit Google offices in Cambridge, MA. The purpose of the trip was to show students interested in computer science what they could potentially do with a computer science degree and present them with an opportunity to learn from some of the best computer scientists in the world.

Students were greeted by three developers—Jessica, Adam, and Dan—from Google, and they presented us with a brief background of the company and an overview of Google's history. We toured several areas of the office, and students made note of the lack of cubicles and the transparent working environment. Employees were not isolated from each other, nor did walls partition them. Workspaces were open and visible, enabling a collaborative environment. Employees moved around freely and took occasional snack breaks.

Students also took note that Google employees are never too far from food and that the food choices were color coded for their nutritional value. When it came time for lunch later in the day, students were impressed by the abundance of healthy choices available for lunch. However, it was sushi day, so most students opted for the mac and cheese.

Not long into the tour one student asked, "Why are schools so disconnected from how people work on a daily basis? Why can't schools look more like this office?" I didn't have an immediate answer because I have been pondering the same question for years. I reminded this student that a Google office is a small sample of how things occur on a daily basis at most companies, but I reinforced how committed Google is to providing the best environment for productivity and efficiency for all of its employees. Apparently Google is on to something.

After the tour, students sat down in a conference room with three Google developers and a Chrome OS developer to brainstorm their ideal computer science course. Before we started, I shared with students that we were in the drafting phase of putting together a hybrid course, tentatively titled "Google Academy," that will be co-taught by the three Google developers in the room and a Burlington High School teacher.

Here is the draft of the course description.

Google Academy: A Hybrid Learning Experience

Professors:

Meeting Time: TBD and online M-F

Meeting Location: TBD

Course Number: TBD (500–900)

Course Description

The Google Academy will be a unique experience that examines a variety of topics in computer science and explores several languages such as Python, C++, Visual Basic, etc. Beyond the programming aspect of the course, students will participate in an authentic, collaborative environment that promotes transparent, engaged learning. Students will learn first hand what it takes to work and thrive in a major company while learning how to manage time and projects independently.

This course will commence both online and face-to-face. The Google Academy will be co-taught by multiple Google programmers and one Burlington High School teacher. The course will also require bi-weekly participation at the Google offices in Cambridge. The Google Academy will require the students to work independently, responsibly and manage their time and assignments throughout the duration of this course.

Learning Pathways

Since this is a hybrid-learning course, primarily taught remotely, each student will set out on a unique pathway throughout the course. Initially, students will be introduced to the structure of hybrid learning environments and the expectations that come with this type of learning.

DESCRIPTION COMPLETION
Pathway 1
Pathway 2
Pathway 3
Pathway 4

Hybrid Learning Expectations

1. Students must maintain a daily journal that will chronicle their progress and serve as the reflective piece of this course. There are no defined length or content requirements; however, students should synthesize their learning with their progress and the products they create. Moreover, this journal will be a living, sustainable history of students' learning. Secondly, the journal will serve as a digital resource that will explain a process or a programming language. Students will then organize pieces of their daily journal on a wikispace.

2. Each student will embark on a learning pathway selected by the student. Once a learning pathway is determined, students will work toward a goal set forth by the student and approved by the professors. Each student will submit a learning pathway proposal to the professor.

3. The learning pathway proposal will serve as the binding agreement

between the student and the professor that will guide the student through the first few weeks of the course. This learning pathway proposal must include the following items:

 a. Goal or objective
 b. Expectations of the student during the pathway
 c. Timeline for completion
 d. Answers the question: How will my work contribute to the greater good of society and innovation?
 e. Demonstration method

4. At the conclusion of each learning pathway, students will be required to assemble a panel for a demonstrative presentation. Students must have two faculty members and one administrator present for their pathway demonstration. Each student should write letters to their prospective panelists addressing the subject, date and time of the demonstration. Students must also complete an abstract for each pathways demonstration.

5. Before submitting letters to prospective panelists, students must author an abstract for each learning pathway demonstration they conduct throughout the semester. The abstract should consist of one, concise paragraph that touches upon the specifics of their pathway demonstration.

Grading

Students will be graded on the content of their daily journals, their progress in their learning pathways and ultimately, in their learning pathway demonstration.

TYPE	CRITERIA FOR GRADE	100-90	89-80	79-70	69-0
Journal	Each week the student presents thorough journal entries that serve as a intuitive timeline of the work each student is completing. The journal is specific, comprehensive and reflects on an ultimate theme or goal. Student displays proficiency in the conventions of the English language to convey the innovative process.				
Participation and progress	The student completes his or her journal on a regular basis, communicates regularly with the professors and uses hybrid learning time effectively. Effective use of time can be seen in the journal and reinforced in the product goal each student has set forth.				

(Continued)

Pathway Demonstration	The pathway demonstration presents a comprehensive look at the student's learning progress from beginning to end goal. The student may have not met the desired goal, but presents evidence for falling short of the goal and a prospectus for reexamining that goal in the next phase of the course. The student's presentation meets the learning objective or goal set forth by the student and approved by the professors and addresses the question: *How will my work contribute to the greater good of society and innovation?*

Source: Groton-Dunstable Regional School District

Once we described the potential course, we asked the students how they wanted to structure the course and what they wanted to learn. Students began listing areas of interest in the context of computer science, ranging from open source coding to coding games and iOS applications. It was great to hear students discuss what *they* wanted to learn as opposed to hearing what they *have* to learn.

Students generated ideas that filled two whiteboards. The room was filled with conversation and questions. It was rewarding to sit back and watch students casually interact with these engineers and ask them questions about what it takes to get to where they are in their careers. It was one of those moments as an educator where you see the great potential for our schools and our students.

Students left excited and eager to hear more about the course that they just helped design. They were also excited about the free Pepsi "Next" they obtained from the vendor on the street pitching the new soft drink to pedestrians.

I'm excited that my district and administration are open to the opportunity for connecting with the business sector to give our students a purposeful learning experience. I'm grateful for the connection I made with three generous Google employees willing to volunteer their time to guide our students through this course. I hope this is a trend that catches on in the education community—a trend that enables more schools to embrace, not limit, technology opportunities that connect students with the community and provide purposeful learning experiences.

Reflecting on the evolution of the student Help Desk course makes me proud. The students who had the opportunity to take this course not only learned about technology in education, but they also have developed critical thinking skills, writing skills, troubleshooting skills, and customer service skills. Some Help Desk students went on to majors in information technology, computer science, and so on. Other students pursued concentrations completely outside of technology. Regardless of their path, they received an experience that touched upon a variety of skill sets.

This course and its effectiveness come down to a simple word that I have mentioned several times in this text: trust. Sometimes it's not easy for adults to realize that students, in some regards, know more about a specific subject than they do. Personally, I've learned a lot from the Help Desk students I have encountered. They never ceased to impress our school community and me. I encourage you to borrow or adapt the resources I have included in this chapter and propose this course in your district. Also, this is not solely limited to secondary students (9–12). In both of my experiences, this course was adapted by each middle school. I could even envision this course working at the elementary level with some major differences in access and focus. Regardless of the grade level, take the time to strongly consider adopting a student-led Help Desk course. The benefits will resonate across the district and serve as a viable support line for district and school technology issues.

ENDNOTES

1. http://bpsedtech.org/
2. http://edcampxedu.org/
3. https://twitter.com/dvillanojr
4. http://www.mobileaware.com/
5. https://bitbucket.org/rleonard/chromebook-scanning-app/overview

CHAPTER

6

Sustaining Digital Communities

- **Embrace trust and transparency with your teaching**
- **What does it mean to be a connected educator?**
- **Engaging with social and digital spaces**

There's a phrase from a video[1] that describes what Creative Commons is that I commonly use when describing what I aspire a school culture to be: "A Shared Culture of Learning."

This phrase defines what a school culture should be and can be if it's not quite there yet. It reinforces the importance of working together for a common goal and for providing the best strategies for teaching and learning. One of the ways I've helped bring this phrase to life is by integrating new technologies and applications to connect teachers, students, and community. But, it doesn't stop at providing hardware and software. It means building bridges within a school community that leverage these technologies and applications at a pace that is comfortable for everyone involved. For some it will be exploring a blog and possibly Twitter, for others it will be attending our Thursday EdTech Genius Bar or a conference. The point to remember is that connected educators are not just the educators you see blogging and tweeting, but also the ones you see developing offline connections.

What I have been witnessing at Groton-Dunstable Regional School District is a school community anxious to integrate new technologies and design new paradigms for teaching and learning. And, this is happening in part by bringing our teachers together each Thursday for an optional EdTech Genius Bar. Teachers are not simply jumping into the Twitter waterfall in order to be a connected educator; rather, they are physically connecting and sharing beyond our Thursday events.

Again, this transition will run smoothly if school leadership allows it to happen. What's more, this transition shouldn't be focused on applications or hardware but on conversations. Simply giving teachers time to discuss and then share best practices around EdTech will elevate the use in the classroom.

One of the big misconceptions is that in order to create a shared culture of learning every staff member must join the social media race. While Twitter, Google+, Facebook, and MOOCs (massive open online courses) are all great opportunities to expand access to connections, resources, and opportunities, bringing teachers together offline is priceless.

The offline world is where I, personally, have made some of my strongest connections. Many of these connections started with social media use, but they elevated when I made the offline connections. I attended conferences like EduCon[2] in Philadelphia that is hosted yearly by the Science Leadership Academy students and Principal Chris Lehmann. I attended and hosted several Edcamps in the past few years and continued to make and strengthen connections during these events. It's imperative for educators to connect in some way in both worlds. I am grateful for making connections on Twitter and through my blog. It's opened many doors for me. I am equally grateful that I attended these conferences and went beyond my computer screen to connect with the educators I've met online.

I've always said that at its core, technology integration is about access and opportunities that might have otherwise not been available. The other great innovation that has taken place is that teaching is no longer a job done in isolation. Teaching can happen almost anytime, and anywhere. The rise of online education and virtual learning opportunities has provided validation and credibility for these paradigms. But what does it really mean to be a connected educator? The goal is not to have a Twitter account with 500,000 followers, but rather to understand the power of the medium and use it to share and highlight what you and your students are doing. Building your network and, inevitably, your brand is something that has almost become essential in education and the rest of the workforce.

To highlight this point, I'd like to share a blog post that I wrote a few years ago. I just lost my job abruptly at the hands of a charter school looking to slash talent (four teachers and the principal) in order to integrate cheaper, Teach for America employees. Upon finding out this information, I didn't know where to turn. The only thing at the moment that made sense for me was my blog and Twitter. There, I had made connections and knew that if I spoke people would hopefully respond. The scenario is also something I have used numerous times to share the power of these mediums and how they can be used in a positive light. Many times the stigma around social media is dark, and the media only highlight instances when it goes awry. However, I'd like to take this opportunity to share this post in its entirety.

I arrive at school for a meeting with our CEO. I assume it is a meeting about the upcoming conference that I am holding at his school, ntcamp. I sit down and he begins telling me that our budget is in disarray and that my instructional technology position that I created and began implementing into the school needs to be cut out of the budget. This is sad news, however, I assumed I could still work as an instructional technology coordinator throughout the school while teaching my classes. I had basically assumed the role as ITC for the past year; helping teachers integrate technology with their curriculum. So, I figured I would be teaching the AP English Language and Composition and returning to my regular teaching duties (NOTE: I just returned back from the AP conference in DC. The School paid for the ticket). I created the syllabus and was in the process of submitting it to the College Board for approval and had also set up a summer reading network via a wikispace and blogger. Students were reading, responding to prompts, and then blogging about them. All of the blogs were linked to the wikispace and it was a well-oiled machine.

I ask what classes I will be teaching next year along with the AP courses. He responds with, "We are getting someone else to teach AP." Wait. . . . WHAT!? Why? This makes no sense. I have the most teaching experience in the English Department and now you are telling me that I can't teach the course I created? Plus, I can't teach at all?

In short, the school's budget did not include the contract I had signed. I leave the office confused, upset, and bewildered. In a few short minutes I went from having two dream teaching positions to having nothing. I could not make sense of this. I told several colleagues that were in school that day teaching and their facial expressions said it all. No one could make sense of it. A few hours later another colleague of mine encountered the same shock and awe conversation. She was the History Department Chair and in my opinion, and most of the students' opinion, one of the most well-respected and well-liked teachers in our building.

In the span of an hour my school said good-bye to seventeen years of

(Continued)

teaching experience. They preferred to have brand new Teach for America teachers replace us. In the sports world this makes sense. You go with youth over experience, but not in education.

Moving on . . .

I have started moving on from my former school and am in the process of seeking out the next path. This journey began on Saturday when I hosted and organized my first unconference at the same school that had just let me go. Not only did I speak positively about the school throughout the entire day, but I promoted their efforts and accomplishments. I have nothing bad to say about my school. They provided so many opportunities for me to grow as an educator and I feel I made a valuable contribution to advancing their curriculum and highlighting ways in which students and teachers can integrate technology more efficiently. I did not want to bring this news with me to ntcamp because I wanted ntcamp to shine like no other. I put every ounce of my energy into making ntcamp the best conference for all in attendance and I am already working towards the next version. ntcamp became my only focus and a welcomed distraction from reality.

If you are going to lose your job it helps to have a Personal Learning Network behind you to pick you up and get you back on track. I recognize the fact that many people are struggling with joblessness in our country and this can happen to anyone. The value and support of a PLN will only make this occurrence easier and reinforce that we are never in this business of teaching alone. It also helps to have a conference waiting for you that weekend where the majority of your PLN will be in attendance. I made a lot of great connections at ntcamp and learned a lot throughout the day. I sit back and smile at all the great comments that have been circulating about ntcamp and am truly excited for more unconferences throughout the year. Thank you to everyone who made ntcamp a shining example of how professional development and personal learning networks can create valuable learning for teachers and in turn benefit all of our students.

Oh, one more thing, if you know of any open positions get in touch with me.

Source: http://www.andrewmarcinek.com/2010/07/resume-and-references-available-upon_27 .html

And they did get in touch with me. This happened in 2010 and three years later, as a result of continuing to stay connected, work tirelessly, and never settle, I write this sentence as the director of technology for a school district. This outcome is no guarantee, and a lot must fall into place in order for it to happen, but it's a possibility. The takeaway from this story and many others like it is that making digital connections and using digital spaces to amplify your teacher voice can lead to amazing opportunities. The next few subchapters will introduce the reader to some ideas to not only connect yourself as an educator, but how to connect your students to great content and a broader audience.

THE BEST TECHNOLOGY IS GOOD TEACHING

We have reached a point in education technology where devices are, for the most part, adaptable. Most of the programs a school uses throughout a typical day are web-based and hardly anything is stored locally. At Burlington Public Schools, our director of instructional technology, Dennis Villano, likes to take someone's iPad and make the motion as if he were going to smash it into a million pieces.

This hypothetical simulation is a great example of how little hardware actually matters any more. While both the iPad camp and the Chromebook camp will argue how their respective device is superior, I can easily envision both working well for a variety of content-area classrooms. In fact, the idea of going all in with a singular device is beginning to evolve. What school districts and administrators should control are the ways in which they create and foster a culture of adaptability before instituting a 1:1 environment.

As I mentioned earlier, the best device a school can roll out is a teacher who can adapt to new and emerging technologies, does not always require formal training for learning and staying current, and is not tethered to a product (such as PowerPoint or a SMART Board) in order to teach. Education technology will continue to progress, and part of this evolution will be for students and teachers to stay current with both curriculum and digital literacy. Even in the absence of technology, a great teacher will continually seek out ways to engage his or her students in great lessons, simulations, or challenges.

To illustrate the points I've made, I'll share a true story. A few years ago, our high school had a visitor from Perth, Australia. She expected to see iPads being used to engage and instruct, but what she actually saw were fly swatters. Yes, fly swatters.

We walked into Todd Whitten's class and witnessed two students at the front of the board slapping fly swatters over terms projected on the wall. The concept was novel, yet effective. Some students were using their iPads to record the review via Evernote, while others watched their classmates have a debate at the board over the subject at hand. Basically, Whitten was providing a prompt, students had to slap the term on the board that coordinated with that prompt, and then discuss or debate their reasoning. Regardless of the devices or applications, the students were engaged. And I am certain there are many other classrooms out there like Whitten's. I'm certain that the use of technology can be veiled by innovative learning goals and objectives. I'm certain that Whitten did not need mandatory training on the technology he and his students were using at the moment to create an engaging lesson.

The simple point is that Whitten can adapt to the environment and challenges he faces as an educator—which is why his classroom desk design is never the same. He not only adapts personally to new and emerging technologies and teaching strategies, but he also challenges his students to adapt to different classroom designs daily. This is what being a "21st century educator" should look like.

Contrary to my assertion is the sentiment that teachers don't have enough time to learn new things, or that professional development must come during contracted hours approved by a union. And that is fine. Eventually these "educators" will be replaced as quickly as the technologies and progressive pedagogy (alliteration breakdown: say it five times fast!) they refute or hold onto for dear life. What will sustain through all the changes is the teacher who is constantly curious, driven by the possibilities of his or her classroom, and never satisfied with repeating lessons and practice. Devices come and go, but progressive teachers who adapt will last longer than any device.

Here are some options for self-paced, learn-when-you-can professional development. Your district will not hand you these options, but I encourage you to seek out these digital learning communities.

ITUNES U

iTunes U is an iPad-based repository of courses, lectures, and resources for teachers and students. The content can be accessed exclusively on the iPad, and the material is all vetted for accuracy and copyright. Courses can be accessed or created by individuals or teachers through iTunes U Course Manager.[3] Course Manager is only available on the Apple platform and when using the Safari browser.

COURSERA

Coursera[4] is a free online course catalog that allows anyone in the world to take courses from some of the best instructors on the planet. Coursera does not offer accreditation for teachers yet, but they are advocating for this issue. Regardless, this site is chock full of courses that anyone can take at any time.

GOOGLE+

Google+ is emerging as a credible venue for professional development and anytime learning. It's a free platform, and if you work in an organization that employs Google Apps for Education, you already have an account. Google+ offers Google "Hangouts" as the venue for presenting professional development sessions. The best part about this option is that Hangouts are archived on the YouTube account of the author or group.

TWITTER

Everyone in education *loves* Twitter. Twitter can be a great venue for learning if you organize it and filter it (I recommend TweetDeck). Jumping headfirst into something like #edchat will only confuse and overwhelm you. My recommendation is to use Twitter sparsely at first. Find a few educators to follow, and spend a good amount of time listening, reading, and processing. Follow Steve Anderson, Kristen Swanson, Alec Couros, John Spencer, Lyn Hilt, Rich Kiker, Dean Shareski, Joyce Valenza, Kyle Pace, and Edutopia—to start. But start simple and listen to what the aforementioned educators have to say.

BECOMING A CONNECTED EDUCATOR

FIND YOUR DIGITAL SPACE

I've been sharing ideas on a blog since 2008. Right, I'm cool. But really, sharing information is a powerful thing. Sharing through digital spaces is not only efficient, economical, and convenient, but it's super powerful. It's hard to comprehend, but I've shared something nearly every day since social networks developed and became readily available. What's more, I've shared nearly everything in my teaching career via a blog, Twitter, or Google+. At this juncture, if you're not sharing what you're doing digitally, you're missing out on some great ideas happening in education and within other contexts. As educators, we no longer have to work in isolation.

So here are some ideas and some ways to elevate your digital space.

FIND A PLATFORM—BLOGGER VS. GOOGLE SITES

This is probably the most mind-numbing part of the process. You could be in a room of 10 people and they would all recommend something different. My two cents: It depends on what you want to share, how frequently you want share, and your audience.

If you want to stick within your Google Apps for Education ecosystem, then these platforms are one way to go. Also, if you plan on posting daily, or weekly, this is the platform for you. A blog is intended for periodic information, and a website is for static information that may change occasionally. Consider Blogger to be your newsletter 2.0. Groton-Dunstable Regional High School Principal Mike Mastrullo uses Blogger[5] to present updates and share information about what is happening at the school. Parents subscribe via e-mail and receive an e-mail alert anytime Mastrullo posts something to his blog. Plus, parents can bookmark his blog site and have a single reference point rather than searching through e-mails.

Like Blogger, Google Sites will also allow you to remain in the Google Apps for Education ecosystem. Plus, Sites gives you the opportunity to collaborate and share within your grade-level teams or with your students. For example, our fourth-grade team at Florence Roche Elementary School is building one site, but teachers have their own page that they can construct. Sites can remain private if necessary, and teachers can invite only those they wish to the website. This is important to remember depending on your school's AUP and publishing rights forms.

Unlike Blogger, Google Sites serves as a collaborative digital space and a way to share and house static information. Blogger, or a blog, is meant to be updated periodically. For example, Florence Roche Elementary's principal, Liz Garden, updates her blog every Monday morning.[6] It includes a topical post along with information about what she is reading, events happening in her school, informal classroom observations, and resources that she's found. This blog not only serves as a great resource for the Florence Roche school community, but it is a professional portfolio for Garden and her great work as principal.

Google Sites also serves as a strong option for teacher and student digital portfolios; a Groton-Dunstable Regional High School independent study student created such a site with Google Sites.[7] It's also important to note that the final product was not a directive; the student simply saw that the technology was available and leveraged it to make her portfolio shine.

DEVELOP YOUR BRAND

After you select your platform, the next phase is branding yourself and your digital space. Within the context of an educational digital space, it's best to be consistent about what you share, the tone of your writing, and the topics you cover. For example, it's probably not the best idea to share information on the great things happening at your school one week and then follow up with a diatribe about how Common Core is destroying the youth of America. It's best to stay on a steady path with a consistent theme or message.

Again, Liz Garden and Mike Mastrullo do a really good job of this by presenting a consistent tone in their writing, staying on topic with a theme, and organizing their posts and their blogs in a way that is appealing to the school community.

SHARE IT

"If you make something and don't share it, was it made?"

Mark Hatch, CEO Techshop

Digital spaces and platforms, in conjunction with social media, have allowed us to share our work to a greater audience. Educators, who once lived and worked in an isolated environment—within their district, within their schools, within their departments—now have the ability to not only share resources and information but also consume and integrate what others are sharing.

Like finding a platform for your digital space, finding a consistent place to share is also important. I share consistently to three social networks: Facebook, Google+, and Twitter. However, when you start, it's best to stick with one and branch out as you progress down this path. I started with Twitter, found common hashtags,[8] and eventually created a network of educators that I connected with via Twitter or who I had met at a conference or workshop.

At Groton-Dunstable, we created our own hashtag—#gdrsdchat—and use it to connect our students, teachers, and greater school community. I would highly recommend this and encourage staff to start off working within your school's common hashtag before swimming out into deeper water. It's a good, comfortable learning environment and takes the idea of personal learning communities to a new level and space. We also posted a #gdrsdchat hashtag widget on the front page of our district's website. This is another way of sharing information and resources about our school community.

A digital space is extremely important for an educator. It not only provides the user with a limitless place to organize and share his or her thoughts and information, but it also serves as a living archive.

WHY SHOULD I BLOG?

The term "blog" is thrown around a lot in education. In the last five years, blogs have become a public voice for many educators. Blogs allow teachers to share and connect with others. Teachers can subscribe to other educators' blogs and see how another teacher is teaching *Hamlet* in North Dakota. Education blogs have evolved from "here's what I think about everything" to a place where educators can share their educational practices, make meaningful connections with other educators, and reflect on the work they have done over the course of the year. Blogs have become an open source curriculum binder that helps all educators connect, share, and grow professionally.

Since October is Connected Educator Month[9] (I didn't even know this was a thing, but cool), I felt this would be a good subject to cover. With that said, here are some ideas on how to get started.

1. Find a platform. This is probably the easiest part of the blogging process. It's equivalent to picking out an outfit for the day. You're tied to that shirt and tie combination, but you know you can change it if you'd like. In short, don't spend a lot of time dwelling on the platform or the theme.

The two primary blogs that I see are from Blogger or WordPress. I'd venture to say these two are the industry standard, but who likes standards?

Blogger offers a simple setup process for users, and if your school has Google Apps for Education you already have an account set up and waiting for you. If you don't have a Google Apps for Education environment, you can simply create a Blogger .com account for free.

WordPress is not tied to any particular e-mail or environment, and it is free as well. WordPress also offers premium accounts that include purchasing your domain. This option is available for both Blogger and WordPress accounts. The difference is in the address. For example:

Own the domain: andymarcinek.com

Free domain blogger: andymarcinek.blogspot.com

Free domain WordPress: andymarcinek.wordpress.com

2. Define your message. Once you have your blog set up, you want to design a format and goal. Basically, who is your audience and what do you want to give them? Some examples:

- **Communicate to parents and students**—Have your parents and students subscribe to your blog by e-mail. This way every time you post, they will receive it in their e-mail. This system allows parents to get updates on what is happening in the classroom and for administrators to relay what's happening at the school. It's a great way to reach out to the community and allow them to see what's happening.

- **As a classroom webpage**—I've used a WordPress blog as my primary classroom page for the past few years, and it's worked great. It's allowed me to archive old assignments and reflect on what I did, as well as what my students accomplished throughout the year. Plus, it's a centralized location for information that students can access almost anywhere.

- **As a personal reflection page**—Sometimes you just want to share your thoughts or an idea that you'd like feedback on from your network. I've used this format to share both professional and personal items in my career and my life. I honestly feel that the constructive, honest feedback has been wonderful. Plus, for me, writing about personal moments in my life, whether it be of sadness or joy, has been therapeutic for me and also for other members of my personal learning network. In short, it's a good thing to share and accept feedback.

3. Enjoy and share the process. Blogging is both a selfish and selfless act and, many times, thankless. Blogging is a good process for educators to get in the habit of doing. It's a time for us to reflect on our work and possibly garner feedback that we can use to make our work and us better.

Blogging is also a selfless, thankless act. When we blog, we place ourselves on the stage for others to see and respond to directly. It's also a place that no one may show up to. And that's fine. We shouldn't blog for fame, awards, or royalties from AdWords, but simply because sharing is a good thing. When we share our learning, our process, or our educational journey, we invariably help others with their learning, their process, and their journey.

TWITTER

Back in the fall of 2013, I, along with many other educators, had the unique opportunity to connect with US Secretary of Education Arne Duncan on Twitter. Tom Murray organized the chat via the #edtechchat hashtag. Around 8 p.m., Secretary Duncan made his way into the chat column and the barrage of tweets ensued. For someone trying to break into Twitter, this was probably not the best forum; however, it did show the impact connecting this way could have.

As the chat continued, Secretary Duncan began asking questions using the Q1—A1 format. Users prefaced their tweets with A1 (based on the question number) and ended each one with the hashtag #edtechchat. Following the chat was nearly impossible in real-time as tweets cruised down the screen in a frenzied manner. Occasionally I tried to retweet a good question or comment someone posted, but overall it was hard to keep pace.

Eventually, I posed a question to Secretary Duncan in which he was kind enough to reply. Once this happened, I felt pretty cool. I had to explain to several people how we actually connected and that it was legit and that I didn't actually know Secretary Duncan, but we now shared a brief connection in time. This occurrence also caused me to reflect momentarily on the connections and opportunities that I've had since joining Twitter five years ago.

I don't think Twitter is the key ingredient to being a connected educator, nor do I feel it's required for someone to be a connected educator. My point is

> **Andrew P. Marcinek** @andycinek 5m
> A4: @arneduncan How has connecting tonight and prior provoked your thinking and influenced decisions in your career? #edtechchat

> **Arne Duncan** ✔
> @arneduncan
>
> @andycinek Helps me look at issues from multiple perspectives and better understand their complexity. #edtechchat
>
> 10/28/13, 8:41 PM

Source: Arne Duncan

that Twitter can be a really great thing and provide many of us with access to opportunities we otherwise may not be privy to. As educators, we should make connections regardless of the medium. Edcamps, conferences (local and national), and learning communities within a district are great ways to connect as well. Jumping into the social media ring will simply heighten those offline connections and broaden the scope of your learning.

If you decide you want to get into Twitter, I will suggest a few steps that I share with anyone who asks me about it.

1. Once you set up your account, encourage a few colleagues to join as well. Develop a "hashtag" for your cohort and share a few things with each other using the hashtag. This will expose you to ways in which you can share, filter, and organize your Twitter experience.

2. Download TweetDeck for Mac or PC. There are a lot of Twitter applications out there, but my preference has always been TweetDeck. Mobile platforms will be different, but the Twitter app for iPhone is probably the best way to go.

3. Organize. One of the great features about Twitter is that you can tailor it directly to your liking. Lists are a great way of organizing people (i.e., English teachers) and what they share online. I've created lists and then I can easily browse through those lists, whether it's on the mobile or desktop platforms. Before you tweet, organize!

4. I would suggest limiting your involvement initially in Twitter chats. They can be overkill for even the most experienced user and can sometimes be an echo chamber of pithy platitudes. The key is to organize first and spend a good amount of time listening, lurking, and absorbing what you see. Twitter is a place where you can simply consume; however, it's always better to share. My suggestion would be to start a small hashtag chat within your school community and then branch out into larger chats like #edchat.

5. "Don't take Twitter too seriously." This is a great piece of advice from Dean Shareski,[10] who has been sharing on Twitter for a while. Twitter can be a conversation, it can be a resource, and it can be funny. We all need to laugh a little, but we must maintain a healthy balance between professionalism and over-sharing cat videos. Plus, don't get caught up with pseudo-celebrity Twitter hierarchy of educators. One hundred thousand followers does not always equal credibility. Again, Twitter is most useful when it is organized. Follow people who you have read, connected with in person, or who are simply good at sharing quality information and are occasionally funny.

Over the years I've learned and gained a lot from connecting on Twitter. It's a community that allows me the flexibility to ask a question or have a conversation with people all over the world anytime, anywhere. This medium has had an impact on my life, my friends, and my career. The key in all of this is to share what you do and highlight your teaching, your school, and your district whether you are on Twitter or offline with colleagues. My brief connection with Secretary Duncan won't change or reform educational policy across the country, but it reinforces the power of this medium. Secretary Duncan may not enact or change anything based on the Twitter chat, but it shows us all he is listening. That's a powerful connection.

GOOGLE+ AND HANGOUTS

Since I started in education, I have been trying to find ways to connect students' learning beyond the classroom walls. Initially, the task presented many hurdles. Infrastructure was limited, devices were bulky and slow, and the access was not quite available. In order to connect students with the outside world, a permission slip and a school bus were needed. Today, many of those hurdles have been overcome, and connecting students beyond the classroom is a viable option. To make those connections, I use Google Hangouts.

Hangouts, the social media feature of the Google+ platform, are online spaces offering teachers and students a great forum to connect with one or many participants and engage in a real-time dialogue. If you are a school that uses Google Apps for Education, then all of your teachers have the ability to set up their own Google+ page and use the Hangouts feature. I have seen examples of department meetings taking place via Google Hangouts and noticed a growing number of online presentations happening via this forum.

One of the many reasons I like Google Hangouts is for the ability to broadcast a talk live and then archive that broadcast. My students and I have been asked to present our Help Desk course at several conferences, as well as participate in interviews through this feature. Most recently my students connected with the ACTEM conference in Maine.[11] While we would have enjoyed attending this conference in person, there were too many scheduling conflicts. So I connected with Alice Barr and we set up a Google Hangout. When I presented with my students, we broadcast the Hangout so that everyone sitting at the conference could see and hear us, and we also connected with those who were simply browsing their Google+ page or Twitter. Additionally, we were able to archive the presentation to share with others.

Besides having the option to incorporate a pirate hat and a monocle while video conferencing via a Google Hangout, participants have the ability to quickly share screens for demonstrations, incorporate the Google Drive suite of apps for collaborative work, and collaboratively watch and discuss a YouTube video through the Google Hangout box. Again, all of these talks can be archived and saved directly to your YouTube account for future reference.

I see many opportunities for students and teachers using Google Hangouts in the classroom. Recently, my Help Desk students presented their TED Talk research projects via a Google Hangout. This gave us the ability to broadcast and archive student presentations while sharing them with a wide audience. Students were not only receiving feedback from one person, but they also had the ability to reach many. As the course unfolded, my Help Desk students presented bimonthly Google Hangout talks on education technology and how it affects student learning. Students created scripts, configured a small set, and worked with camera angles to bring their shows to life. Each student pitched a show to his or her teams, wrote a script for that 10-minute show, and then filmed it live via a Google Hangout. They hope to reach many viewers and connect with students and teachers globally to share their ideas and make meaningful connections through this medium.

With Google Hangouts, the possibilities for classroom integration are infinite. Once teachers discover the simplicity of this application, they will begin to see the opportunity and value it has for classroom engagement. Professionally, I see it as a great opportunity to connect and share my ideas with a vast audience. This summer, Burlington Public Schools will begin offering weekly Google Hangouts for our Tuesday free professional development sessions. Over the past two years we have opened our doors to anyone who wanted to visit and learn about anything related to education and EdTech integration. Initially, we had many of our own staff members show up from 9:00 a.m. to noon every Tuesday. Last summer we connected with Abbie Waldron and her EdCamp Summer[12] crew at Wamogo Regional High School via Skype. And this summer we will open our doors a little wider to expand our reach and to create more meaningful conversations and connections.

When it comes to technology and education, I feel the message is quite simple: Technology gives us the ability to connect, share, and learn like never before. Google Hangouts bring all of these verbs together and provide teachers and students a simple, free learning space.

EDCAMPING

One of the hallmarks of an Edcamp is the ability to choose your own adventure. The model allows everyone to participate and have a voice. Nothing is mandated. And, no one is tweeting that they are "giddy" about seeing *"Insert so-called Twitter Celebrity."* There are no over-priced keynote speakers, and vendors are not hounding you. Instead, everyone is giddy (*I promise, last time*) to learn, to share, and to listen.

And, before I go further, I understand that the critic would argue that there is no research to prove an Edcamp is an effective model of professional development.

However, leave it alone. Participants leave an Edcamp feeling good, refreshed, and eager to get back to work on Monday with practical ideas that are available to integrate. That is all the data you need.

One of the misnomers with an Edcamp is that it is a tech conference, or rather, that it is driven by sessions geared toward education technology. This is false. While an Edcamp incorporates a fair amount of technology for promoting and sharing, the sessions really don't require any technology. If you take a moment to observe the surroundings at an Edcamp, you will notice lots of conversations. Sure, there always some people looking at a screen, but more often than not that screen time was for notes or to share.

In fact, the best technology integration at an Edcamp is the ability to share and to listen. This is why the Edcamp model thrives and continues to grow globally—not because everyone is on Twitter or understands how to use an iPad, but rather that everyone is excited to listen, process, and share. This is why Edcamps matter. This is why the Edcamp model works and will sustain for many years to come. This is why participants leave excited to get to work on Monday after giving up a Saturday to learn. And this is why more schools should be having many conversations before considering any piece of hardware. It's the best technology integration you could give your students and teachers.

Regardless of the medium, it's important to share our work as educators. For years educators have worked in isolation or within a department or a school building. What was happening in another district, let alone around the world, was not something that was typically known or sought after. What technology gives our students and us is the ability to connect, share, and learn like no other time in history. There is no downside to sharing your work as an educator.

The resources mentioned in this chapter are a good primer for being a connected educator; however, it is still imperative to develop these digital connections offline. While I have developed a vast resource through a personal learning network, I have managed to stay connected with many members of my network offline. Many of these people I consider close friends. Despite our connection medium, no technology has replaced human interaction. While it's obvious that we can connect, share, and learn in an instant, it's healthy to balance our time online and offline, and engage with both digital and analog resources. Ultimately, this process will yield lifelong learning.

This chapter does not tie directly to a 1:1 school, but it highlights some of the outcomes and opportunities that can burgeon from technology integration. Ultimately, as educators, there should be an inherent desire to learn. There should also be a desire to leverage technology to make connections and share our work to the world. Regardless of the medium we choose, it's important to share our work as educators.

Endnotes

1. https://www.youtube.com/watch?v=1DKm96Ftfko
2. http://educonphilly.org/
3. https://itunesu.itunes.apple.com/coursemanager/
4. https://www.coursera.org/
5. http://gdprincipal.blogspot.com/
6. http://floromondaymorningmusings.blogspot.com/
7. https://sites.google.com/site/digitalportfoliojjdegroot/home
8. http://www.cybraryman.com/edhashtags.html
9. http://connectededucators.org/
10. https://twitter.com/shareski
11. https://www.youtube.com/watch?v=XhZkLmkQUPs&feature=youtu.be
12. https://sites.google.com/a/bpsk12.0rg/Edcamp-tuesdays/home

CHAPTER 7

Dispelling the Myths of EdTech

- **The myths associated with 1:1 environments**
- **Exploring open educational resources (OER)**
- **Options for a paperless classroom**

Technology integration has been happening in schools for years. Every episode, or phase of the device or tool, has changed: some dramatic, some not so much. As I mentioned in the introduction, one of the earliest disruptors in the classroom came in the form of the mounted chalkboard. Regardless of the change, technology, in one form or another, has had a consistent place in our schools throughout time. The constant in this evolution is the teacher. The teacher has always been the key component in the learning process, and he or she has adapted and incorporated technology as time has passed. Some teachers have seen many phases come and go, but they have always found ways to learn and adapt.

From the advent of the chalkboard, to the integration of the iPad, technology has been provoking teachers to reexamine the way they deliver content and transfer information to their students. But, education has never been about technology or devices. It has always been about good teachers who deliver content or information to their students, adaptability, and a progressive mindset.

While many fear the iPad or even Google will take the place of a teacher, I'm certain that day will never come. The human element will always propel the educational system forward, but the medium by which we transfer this information will continue to evolve. And that is what we, as educators, must always embrace.

Technology integration is the ability to highlight the intersection of technology and the content areas. In short, the classroom teacher, who is an expert in his or her field, is still going to command that room with the intellect and array of ideas, but now with a dynamic device in place. While some may argue that both the chalkboard and the iPad are simply tools, I'd like to contend that they both possess highly complex operation systems. In both regards, the teacher has to adapt and change with the technology. And, in doing so, see these inevitable changes as new opportunities to challenge ourselves as learners and provide our students with current resources and technologies.

Technology integration, over time, has provoked teachers to be better and develop new skill sets in the classroom. Although many may see technology as another item on the "to do" list, it's something that keeps us all on our toes and current in our profession. As I mentioned before, technology will never take the place of the teacher; however, it will continually challenge us to be better in a profession that should never dwell in a comfort zone. Teachers, above all, should be the epitome of the constant learner and a consistent example for the students we teach.

It's easy to get caught up or distracted in the reason(s) why your school should take the plunge into the EdTech pool. The impetus behind technology integration has always been, and should always be, to provide students with the best access and opportunities to learning that best model the world that's happening around the school. That's the only reason you need to "sell" your school board, committee, and community on carrying out a technology initiative. It's not about the device, nor is it about the applications associated; simply, it is giving our students access and opportunities to expand their learning.

If that doesn't work, have your students educate the community on why technology in schools is important. I've heard examples of students

- setting up cell phone or smartphone workshops with the elderly;

- hosting tech nights (like I mentioned earlier) to educate and provide support for laptops, iPads, etc.;

- assisting the community with access to resources in local libraries; and

- creating an application that serves the community.[1]

And the list could go on. The point is that technology can bring communities together in great ways. Some would argue otherwise, but bringing technology (in any form) into your school district opens a variety of avenues for students and teachers to explore. While some students see technology integration as a way to better organize their academic careers, other students may see it as an inciting incident that illuminated their passion.

However, as with any new trend or phase, there are rumors, misconceptions, and false statements that affect how programs are carried out. Here are some myths that I have discovered in my practice and my attempt to dispel them.

Dispelling the Myths of 1:1 Environments

MYTH 1: THE DIGITAL GENERATION NEEDS TECHNOLOGY

False. Many talking heads, whether on Twitter or at conferences, feel the need to validate technology integration by deeming it necessary for the next phase of students' lives. While I do believe that technology integration should be part of the educational context, this assertion should not be the reason to incorporate devices and applications into your curriculum. For many students, they will travel to college, sit in a giant auditorium, and listen to lectures. Most of their assessments will be done on Scantron forms and offer no project-based alternative. The most technology that students will encounter in college will be e-mail, word processing (either Microsoft Office or Google Docs), and social media outlets for socializing.

I did not pull this evidence out of thin air. Many students who return from top colleges and universities will list the three technology uses above. They will also detail the limited engagement they encounter in many of their classes. I'm not trying to debate the need for technology integration, but I'm simply stating that it's irresponsible to claim the digital generation "needs" technology.

Technology should not stand out; it should simply blend with dynamic teachers and the engaging curriculum they design. To validate technology integration simply because this generation gets it and needs it is a thin assertion. In fact, many students deemed "digital natives" prefer analog formats for learning and organizing. Integrate technology because you know it is purposeful and helps create engaging learning environments for students.

MYTH 2: THE IPAD IS SIMPLY A TOOL

False. I once read a post about an iPad being compared to one of the simplest tools, a hammer. Comparing an iPad to a hammer is a naive way of thinking about a powerful device. The iPad, along with laptops, Chromebooks, and other tablet options, all boast advanced operating systems with intuitive design. Despite their intuitive design, tasks as simple as taking notes and saving to the cloud can be a struggle for many in the "digital generation." Don't assume the student body will simply adapt to the device and the applications because they fall under the age of 20. Creating a 1:1 environment takes dedicated professional development for staff, parents, and the community, as well as the students who will be using it daily.

MYTH 3: IT'S NOT A DISTRACTION

False. I believed this statement for a while and felt that unimaginative teaching was at fault, but this is not the case. Plus, teachers deserve more credit for consistently trying to create engaging classrooms with the resources they have available in a variety of contexts. When I asked a few students if they were distracted by the iPad, they paused to consider the question before answering.

While they said it wasn't any different than looking out of a window or doodling in the margins of a notebook, the device presented a need for added self-control. One student mentioned his grades started slipping, and he realized that it was the result of added stimulus in the App Store. This student realized his fault and soon deleted many of the gaming apps. He also mentioned that the initial appeal of the device and games wore off. While the transition didn't take place overnight, this student soon recognized the potential for learning and organizing with the iPad.

This story shouldn't serve as evidence for not integrating iPads or any device into your school, but simply to help you realize that, for some students, technology integration will present a challenge to focus. While distractions in the classroom are nothing new, they are enhanced for some students as a result of technology devices. To say that a device such as the iPad is not distracting is silly. However, it takes time and understanding by the students to realize what they've been given.

MYTH 4: CREATING OR PURCHASING TEXTBOOKS FOR THE IPAD IS A GRAND INNOVATION

To say you are eliminating textbooks is easy, but actually doing it and making it meaningful and impactful on learning is the hard part. Many times what happens is that schools acquire devices and simply use them as a digital textbook. While this process cuts the cost of the textbook and provides a digital method for distribution, it doesn't change much. Students are still consuming information much like students did in the 20th century.

This process also is very time consuming, and teachers simply don't have the time on the clock to create an entire textbook from scratch. However, schools can look to create personal learning or development communities that are focused on building content. Many schools offer common planning time among departments, and there is usually time throughout the year for faculty meetings and professional development time. What school leaders can look to create is time for teachers to find open educational resources (OER) and build digital content collectively. The best way to do this is through Apple's iTunes U and Course Manager. These tools will give you the ability to develop and design a digital, interactive syllabus or outline of your course. Teachers can build in applications, videos, audio, books, and so on. Plus, students can access the content directly on their iPad, take notes for all materials, and have discussions directly within the applications. The other option that is great about iTunes U is that there are already thousands of courses created by both K–12 professionals and higher education institutions and professors. The key point in busting this myth is don't buy 1,000 iPads simply to engage in activities and lessons that merely change the medium as opposed to innovating the learning experience.

MYTH 5: GOING 1:1 WITH IPADS TEACHES ONE PRODUCT

False. Many times our EdTech team has been accused of being Apple fanboys and fangirls. While we love Apple design and enjoy the ease of its system, we are not teaching a brand. Our students are learning how to use a device with an advanced operating system that assists with organizing, accessing data in the cloud, connecting, and sharing. These skills are more than just device-agnostic. They teach students how to organize their educational workflow in a 21st-century context.

Many of the applications we suggest that students use are not limited to the iPad. If we decided to eliminate iPads tomorrow and switch to Chromebooks, our students could easily adjust to this transition. Students use Google Drive, Dropbox, Evernote, and Notability as their primary workflow and organizational apps.

And these myths are only a few I have uncovered along this journey. Ultimately, the decision to integrate technology, choose a device, and develop policy and procedures should be a collective effort that includes all stakeholders. I cannot stress that enough. Regardless of the device the district selects, they are simply a medium that provides access to a wealth of resources available on the vast landscape of the web. As I mentioned before, the one misnomer about the iPad is that you need applications to teach. The iPad out of the box is a very powerful tool and offers a wealth of native resources.

ALTERNATIVES TO THE STANDARD

Beyond the teaching and learning opportunities, large-scale or even small-scale EdTech initiatives can provoke change that challenges the standard "business as usual" mentality in school districts. Two changes I have seen that have helped redefine standard practice in education are eliminating textbooks and downsizing printers and paper usage. The first change I will discuss, textbooks, has been a staple in education for decades. The textbook has been the cornerstone of student learning in the classroom and also the foundation by which information is both distributed to and consumed by students. However, with the ability to filter, vet, and organize the Internet, schools integrating robust infrastructures, and the advent and cost-effective nature of mobile technologies, the textbook is finally feeling the pressures of extinction.

Paper, on the other hand, is still a necessary evil and expenditure in education; however, its prowess is waning. With the aforementioned advances in education technology there are plenty of ways to consolidate and create paperless environments. But first, let's consider open educational resources.

OPEN EDUCATIONAL RESOURCES

There's a subtle but steady shift happening in classrooms across the nation. More and more, schools are seeking efficient, cost-effective alternatives to using paper and supporting over-priced textbook companies. One way is by supporting technology in schools. Schools are seeking ways to upgrade and sustain wireless infrastructures and integrate mobile devices that broaden teaching and learning opportunities. Similarly, schools are decreasing their dependency on paper and incorporating digital workflows.

What's exciting about this shift in content curation, creation, and distribution is that it allows teachers opportunities to work with the most current information available and serve as the expert when vetting content. Many new teachers are handed a textbook and curriculum map, and then sent into the classroom. While this process provides structure, it limits current information and assumes that we believe exactly what the textbook company is presenting. This is not to say textbook companies are in the business of writing skewed versions of history, science, or math, but rather that students are provided with one viewpoint on the subject.

Time is the hurdle here. The process I described above gives us both content and time, but it's limiting. The best approach to gaining time is working together and making connections. Digital, collaborative environments such as Wikispaces, Google Sites and Docs, blogs, and so on, allow teachers to connect and share over a common goal anytime, anywhere. The best part is that collaborative spaces don't require a curriculum day or even a room for teachers to engage in a single space and develop digital content in an ongoing process.

Once you narrow down your digital collaboration space, the next hurdle is content. Textbooks and curriculum guides make it easy to grab and go—"fast food" for new and experienced teachers when it comes to content. Many times the act of learning from a textbook or a worksheet is monotonous, mindless work for our students. It's more work than learning and, more often than not, they're following a linear path to an answer. The opportunities for creative exploration and inquiry are limited.

In my classroom experience, what I have found most useful are open educational resources (or OER)—content generated by professionals, academics, and authors who have done some of the work for us. OER provide different viewpoints and angles to content that were previously static and myopic. Many OER sites are curated and maintained by nonprofits that may or may not seek an optional donation. These spaces usually require a username and password, and they offer teachers a space to save, download, and share content with others.

To start, here are some outlets providing open educational resources that teachers can begin exploring, sharing, and integrating relatively quickly.

CURRIKI

Curriki[2] is a website that curates content in a variety of disciplines, highlighting noteworthy teachers and content. Membership is free, and users can sign in with their Google Apps or Facebook account. While Curriki is a nonprofit, it asks users for an optional donation. This site integrates well with the iPad and Chromebook, and documents are available in many formats for easy viewing. Here is a testimonial on their site from Leslie G. Perry, a US-based educator and blogger:

> What makes [Curriki] remarkable is how well it is organized, the rating system to guide educators on their search for curricula, and the interactivity included in every lesson plan provided.

CK-12

The CK-12 Foundation offers FlexBooks,[3] full digital texts that students and teachers can access on multiple devices in PDF, MOBI, and ePub formats. This provides broad access to rich content. Here's more from the CK-12 FlexBooks site:

> Services like CK-12 make it easy for teachers to assemble their own textbooks. Content is mapped to a variety of levels and standards including Common Core. You can start from scratch or build from anything in the FlexBooks library.

CONNEXIONS

Connexions[4] is another free OER offering that allows users to sign up with a username and password to access a variety of modules and collections on multiple devices. Their website tells us:

> Connexions is a dynamic digital educational ecosystem consisting of an educational content repository and a content management system optimized for the delivery of educational content. Connexions is one of the most popular open education sites in the world. Its more than 17,000 learning objects or modules in its repository and over 1000 collections (textbooks, journal articles, etc.) are used by over two million people per month. Its content services the educational needs of learners of all ages, in nearly every discipline, from math and science to history and English to psychology and sociology. Connexions delivers content for free over

the Internet for schools, educators, students and parents to access 24/7/365. Materials are easily downloadable to almost any mobile device for use anywhere, any time. Schools can also order low-cost hard-copy sets of the materials (textbooks).

Content is vetted by major organizations and universities, and is accessible in PDF or ePub formats. And the display quality on an iPad in iBooks is excellent.

SMARTHISTORY

Smarthistory[5] is not only a clever play on words, but it is also a great art history resource. This site features content organized by time period, style, artist, and theme. It's more of a gallery of art history than a textbook. Here's an excerpt from a description of their offerings:

> Smarthistory at Khan Academy is the leading open educational resource for art history. We make high-quality introductory art history content freely available to anyone, anywhere. Smarthistory is a platform for the discipline where art historians contribute in their areas of expertise and learners come from across the globe. We offer nearly 500 videos, and these are being translated into dozens of languages. Dr. Beth Harris and Dr. Steven Zucker created Smarthistory and are the Executive Editors. Videos are also available on Khanacademy.org and the Khan Academy app. Smarthistory and Khan Academy are 501(c)3 not-for-profit corporations.

MIT OPENCOURSEWARE

The MIT OpenCourseWare[6] site offers educators and students access to full courses designed and taught by MIT professors. Users can access the entire course library and the entire course packet. Course packets include video interviews with professors, the syllabus, outlines, readings, assignments, projects, and related resources. Here is a brief synopsis from the site:

> MIT OpenCourseWare (OCW) is a web-based publication of virtually all MIT course content. OCW is open and available to the world and is a permanent MIT activity. Through OCW, educators improve courses and curricula, making their schools more effective; students find additional resources to help them succeed; and independent learners enrich their lives and use the content to tackle some of our world's most difficult challenges, including sustainable development, climate change, and cancer eradication.

OER COMMONS

This site offers educators a place where they can connect and share globally with other educators, and work with the curriculum those educators have shared. OER

Commons[7] offers a vast database of teacher-created curriculum. The content is vetted for credibility and provides citations for reference. Users can sign up for a free account, share their own work, and access and curate their own content.

During my time at Burlington Public Schools, we moved toward opening up our course content and started organizing our faculty-created resources—presentations, assignment sheets, and so on—along with OER options. What we are doing is giving our faculty and our students more ways to connect and share dynamic, developing content. Plus, a digital resource created by teachers in conjunction with OER does not require edition upgrades. What's more, teachers can change and update content when needed. This option gives them full autonomy over their classroom content.

To manage this transition, we started using Net Texts as our content management and distribution application. Net Texts is a free application that has many similarities to iTunes U. It allows our teachers to post content—PDFs, videos, photos, audio, and the like—from their web-based management system directly to the students. Teachers can frontload courses for the year and update at any time. When there is an update, students will receive a red badge on their Net Texts app. Once they sync with the Wi-Fi, they can update the course. The other advantage of Net Texts is that students can use it offline (if no updates are pending) and open posted resources such as PDFs in third-party applications (like Notability).

Teachers like this approach because they have full autonomy over their content, can update it at anytime throughout the year, and can deliver it directly to their students. Students like OER because of the intuitive interface and the ability to connect with their classes, both online and offline. Plus, some of our foreign language students who are traveling abroad can easily stay connected through their iPad and the Net Texts app. This allows students to go out and see the world while participating in their respective classrooms.

Integrating quality content into our classrooms is possible. Many feel that, in the absence of a textbook, teaching is directionless. What needs to be highlighted in this shift is that content-area teachers are hired for their expertise in a specific subject. It is our job as educators not only to deliver content but also to provide our students with multiple lenses for evaluating and processing it.

Integrating open educational resources requires little time and research—and, if done collaboratively, it can be more efficient and effective than if planned in isolation. Part of being a connected educator is the ability to connect with each other as well as connecting our students with rich, dynamic content that provokes their thinking and enhances their learning.

PAPERLESS CLASSROOMS

In 2008, I had the opportunity to work in a school that was the beneficiary of a Classrooms for the Future grant championed by then–Pennsylvania Governor

Ed Rendell. The grant spanned two years and provided an infusion of technology into a school, in bulk. That year, we received laptop carts stocked with 30 Lenovo ThinkPad computers, SmartBoards, digital cameras and camcorders (pre-iPad), headphones, and microphones. It was EdTech utopia! However, it was hard to establish universal motivation behind a program that one day just showed up in the classroom.

Besides the abruptness of this program, I was given the opportunity in my English class to use technologies that I had only dreamed of using. I really had no formal training on these machines and devices, but I had a curiosity to see how I could leverage them in my English classroom.

During one of our professional development days the faculty organized in groups and discussed ways in which we could collectively leverage the new technology that was now at our disposal. During one of my meetings I suggested how I was making an attempt to go paperless in my classroom. My plan was to use Google Docs (which was relatively new and not quite the product it is now) and have students share documents instead of print them and turn them in. The response I got from one colleague stuck with me for many years and served as motivation for everything I've done and accomplished in the years since.

"Andy, the paperless thing sounds great, but you're making us all look bad."

This quote never faded with me, and I have been waging a war on paper ever since. Actually, not, but I like to pretend I am.

Regardless, the sentiment resonated with me. My intention in all my work was to never make anyone look bad. That's a waste of time; however, my goal was to potentially save the district a few dollars and teach my classes in an environment that slightly resembled (at the time) a changing job market that was becoming more and more digital.

Today, as the director of technology, I know what it costs per print, for color, and the ease of printing in an educational institution. In many districts, printing is like shopping in a candy store, where all you have to do is press a button. With both the launch of our iPad initiative at Burlington and the Chromebook/iPad deployment at Groton-Dunstable Regional School District, I was continually asked about printing from these devices. In both cases, the answer was no. In both situations, the answer was not only no, but *no,* and we're going to begin consolidating printing options throughout the district.

We did not set out, in both situations, to be mean or eliminate a resource that many teachers need; rather, we wanted to provoke change that reflects the world in which our students will be entering. Also, we provided an option to replace the technology we were phasing out. Not only did we integrate devices in both instances, but we also included the Google Apps for Education suite in both scenarios. This gave teachers and students an e-mail address, plus Google Drive. These options alone give teachers and students a wealth of opportunities to set up digital workflows.

At Groton-Dunstable, we started with the new technology and Google Apps for Education and followed with upgrading our copier fleet and downsizing our standalone, desktop printers. We also integrated a card-swipe system that allowed teachers the convenience of sending multiple jobs to a high-capacity copier, walking up to the machine to swipe in, and releasing the jobs that he or she wanted.

For both students and teachers, the transition from paper to digital takes time. I always tried to provide help for this transition, but I never pushed too hard. In most cases, I'd help one teacher who was eager to change, and in turn, create the "Macy's window" effect (my term, I think). One teacher would take this on and showcase the awesome work he or she is doing and, eventually, it catches on.

What's more, change like this is not done to make teachers' lives more difficult. As tech integration specialists, coaches, and directors, our job is to make the daily schedule of a teacher easier and more efficient. While integrating new technology for some requires a steep learning curve, the possibilities beyond that will grow exponentially.

Following are three applications that can organize your teaching schedule and turn your classroom into an efficient, digital machine.

E-MAIL

As I mentioned above, e-mail has become a constant in the life of every teacher and administrator. Plus, many students now have e-mail accounts and use this medium to submit work or the occasional excuse. For many teachers, it seems like the e-mails will never stop. And, on top of it all, it's become an expectation that we respond to them in a timely manner. The good news is that there's an app for this. It's simply called Mailbox,[8] and it allows the user to sync with his or her Gmail account and determine how to manage e-mail. One of the benefits of Mailbox is the ability to "snooze" messages and categorize them into lists or "later." Using Mailbox quickly allows teachers to organize their day and receive alerts about e-mails when they have time to get back to them.

Another great feature of the Mailbox app is that it's fully integrated with Dropbox. This feature allows users to attach any Dropbox file directly into an e-mail.

FILES

For years, teachers have "saved as" to the "My Documents" folder on their computers. The idea of saving locally or to a flash drive was, and still is, the norm for archiving curriculum materials or important documents. But what happens when your computer crashes, or your machine needs to be replaced, or you leave the flash drive in your pocket and wash it? You lose a lot of great work. With many schools incorporating better infrastructures along with Google Apps for Education environments, educators need to look no further than Google Drive. Google Drive gives every user 30 GB of shared space, and includes docs, spreadsheets, presentations, folders, forms, and more. Teachers can upload and convert a variety of document types for sharing and collaborating. The user is no longer tied to a single device, but he or she can now access, share, and collaborate on documents from any computer, tablet, or smartphone. While Microsoft Office still has premium features, Google Drive is the only teaching tool you need for organizing your data in the cloud and creating simple workflows within your classroom.

REMEMBERING EVERYTHING

My former colleague Dennis Villano said, "Evernote is my brain." There was hardly a day that I didn't encounter Villano looking at Evernote and either adding items to or crossing them off his lists. And he's not alone in this. Evernote has quickly become my go-to app for helping me to remember everything in my day. I can access it from a variety of places and set alerts or reminders for when I need to do something. Evernote is where I make my lists, take a quick picture to remember something . . . and where I am writing this chapter. Another great feature in Evernote is its ability to remember the web. The web clipper for Google Chrome recently received an upgrade that allows users to not only clip a web page for remembering later but also annotate directly on the page. At Groton-Dunstable Regional School District, we're using Evernote for our teacher evaluation system as well.

One of the big misconceptions about technology integration is that teachers have to learn how to teach all over again. This couldn't be further from the truth. At the core, technology integration can save us time and make us more efficient, organized educators. Instead of pushing back against technology integration, first see what it can do for you.

Integrating technology does not need to be an overwhelming, stressful process. Start with one of the applications I mentioned above. Take a few moments to learn the basic steps and see how incorporating these simple apps can turn your classroom into a model of efficiency. Start by trying a Google Site, and watch how it can easily lead to other tools. See Figure 7.1.

Mastering the basics of Google Site can lead users to exploring other Google Apps that integrate beautifully with Google Sites. In essence, if district leaders focus and pace the integration process, the likelihood that users will begin to explore will be far greater than if it was mandated and forced.

FIGURE 7.1   Google Sites Leads to Integrating Other Google Apps

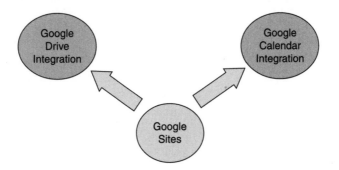

The resources highlighted in this chapter offer a primer for understanding some of the misconceptions associated with 1:1 programs along with alternatives to analog resources. Open educational resources can be a valuable tool for any teacher looking to expand and organize his or her classroom. Plus, these tools offer students a broad perspective. Ultimately, it is our job as educators and district leaders to provide the best access and opportunities for teaching and learning. When we lead with this mindset, our students benefit greatly.

ENDNOTES

1. https://www.youtube.com/watch?v=AWNil_4QIbc&feature=youtu.be

2. http://www.curriki.org/

3. http://www.ck12.org/search/?q=flexbooks&pageNum=1&m=all&at=book

4. http://cnx.org/

5. http://smarthistory.khanacademy.org/

6. http://ocw.mit.edu/index.htm

7. http://www.oercommons.org/

8. http://www.mailboxapp.com/

CHAPTER 8

The Road Ahead

- **Frequently asked questions answered**
- **Conclusions**
- **What's next . . .**

As I mentioned throughout this work, there is no single approach to developing a 1:1 device, a multi-device, or a bring your own device environment. What I've provided are ideas and pieces that district leaders can use to fit their vision in this arena. I'd like to close with some of my most frequently asked questions about technology integration. While the following questions are limited to this text, I am open to dialogue beyond these pages via Twitter and other social media outlets.

HOW DID YOU GET THE FUNDING?

This is probably the most asked question of any I've fielded regarding the two device launches I led. At Burlington, there were several layers to the funding. The first piece of the funding puzzle was the town of Burlington supporting and financing a sweeping infrastructure overhaul of all town and school buildings. So this line item was taken care of at no cost to the school; however, successive budget cycles we made upgrades and installments within our school budget. Infrastructure was seen as a utility for the entire district as opposed to a line item for the Technology Department.

The iPads were purchased with an Apple equity lease that allowed Burlington to pay installments instead of one giant lump sum. The Burlington Middle School iPad launch the following year came in the form of an MSBA project that the district applied for and was granted. This project included the technology, devices, and so on in the cost of the project funding. Again, the funding of 1,000 iPads came at no cost to Burlington Public Schools.

In Groton-Dunstable, I walked into a $562,000 warrant article passed by both towns of Groton and Dunstable to be used for technology upgrades across the district. Groton Power and Light provided $100,000 that was to be used for infrastructure upgrades and installs. The remainder of the money was used to purchase Chromebooks, iPads, projectors, flat-panel TVs and Apple TV units, and new teacher devices. Unlike my experience at Burlington, I had to factor in sustainability with an annual tech budget much lower than $562,000.

Other schools I have worked with, who didn't receive any funding assistance, usually took a staggered approach to tech integration. This came in the form of many classroom pilots that provided data on how the devices were impacting teaching and learning. This is not to say in my two previous experiences data wasn't collected, but it was as important in the decision to integrate more technology.

What Happens to Broken Devices?

During the iPad launch at Burlington High School, we offered students and parents optional insurance for their iPad. In short, the iPad was issued to the student, and the student in conjunction with the parent was in charge of the device. For one year of coverage, students could purchase iPad insurance for $36. This policy covered cracked screens, dropped devices, and so on. The majority of our issues the first year were cracked screens. We also offered students a free case that was provided by the Burlington Chamber of Commerce. Most students purchased their own cases and sought to personalize their device.

Students who did not purchase insurance were responsible for the full replacement cost of the device or the cracked screen. This was articulated before every student received his or her device. Much like a damaged or lost textbook (which cost almost as much as an iPad) students were held responsible for this device. And, we briefed every student and parent on the optional insurance that we would provide through the Worth Ave. Group.

How Were Devices Filtered beyond the School?

During school hours and in accordance with CIPA and COPPA, students' content on the web was filtered. Initially, at Burlington we used the Casper Mobile Device Management (MDM) system to load a profile on every student device. Once installed, this profile allowed us to manage certain elements of the student device.

We had a profile that removed the Safari web browser from the device and replaced it with Lightspeed Mobile Filter. This was only done at the high school, where students took their devices home. The middle school and elementary students did not take their devices home.

The Lightspeed Mobile Browser allowed students to have a filtered web experience in school and beyond our networks. Regardless of the network, the mobile browser we used in place of Safari aligned with our district filters and provided a safe browsing experience for students.

While this process worked well initially, I'd be remiss if I didn't share some of the shortcomings of this model. The Lightspeed Mobile Browser was not efficient or effective. In fact, it slowed students down in their work. The other issue we encountered was that students quickly figured out how to remove the profile from their device. However, we could see if a profile was removed and what apps the student had on his or her device. Eventually we let down our control with filtering devices beyond our networks and recently switched to using the global proxy method with Safari.

Were Social Media Sites such as Instagram, Snapchat, and Facebook a Distraction?

Yes. They are as much of a distraction as a window in a classroom. Social media will always be a distraction depending on how interested a student is in that world. Most students used Snapchat daily. However, we didn't block any social media sites at either Burlington Public Schools or Groton-Dunstable Regional School District.

The reason behind this decision comes in two parts. The first part is that under all federal guidelines, social media sites are not required to be blocked by school districts. The second part is that we provided professional development for teachers on classroom management techniques for having devices in the classroom. For teachers, this was the biggest shift when the devices entered the classroom. In both districts, the tech team continually shared ways for teachers to manage their digital spaces and strategies for students who used devices inappropriately in class. Many of these professional development strategies were mentioned in earlier chapters.

How Much Autonomy Did Students Have to Select Educational Apps That Fit Their Learning Style?

When I was at Burlington High School, we gave our students the freedom to add and subtract apps for their own devices. In our initial presentation to parents and students (before they received their iPads) we briefed parents on several topics that aligned with this question. The first thing we explained was the difference between a free iTunes account and one tethered to a credit card. This choice was ultimately left up to the parents and the students. We recommended that students use a free account and periodically add iTunes gift cards. We also assured parents that students would never need to purchase apps for class. If a teacher wanted to get an app for his or her class, we would go through Apple's Volume Purchase Program (VPP) and load the app onto the device for that class. Each department at the high school had $100 to use for apps; however, there were not many apps purchased.

Additionally, we suggested what we called "Foundational Apps" for students and teachers. These apps were the Mail App, Evernote, Google Drive, and Dropbox. Eventually we added more to this list, but when we first started we briefed parents, students, and teachers that initially these would be the most commonly used applications. And, they were all free. As we progressed through this initiative, we added Explain Everything, Blogger, and Notability; however, we purchased these apps for students.

We also had the "power" to create different profiles for high school students through the Casper MDM system. What this means is that we could create a "lockdown" profile for a student who still needed to use his or her iPad for classes that required it, but take off the App Store, iTunes, the camera, and FaceTime. This was a quick process that could happen on the spot. It was also developed after many conversations with school administrators and how we wanted to proceed with repercussions for inappropriate use.

Our middle school iPads did not go home, and students could not add their own applications. We used Apple's Configurator to push profiles to each cart. Again, we took recommendations from teachers and added the apps accordingly.

How Did Students and Teachers Send and Receive Assignments with Devices?

This was one of the biggest transitions that developed as a result of both districts I mentioned integrating more devices across the K–12 landscape. Also, in both Burlington and Groton-Dunstable, the districts were making efforts to reduce printers and paper use. The annual costs for paper are staggering; consider how much of that cost could be figured into providing educational tools and support.

The biggest driver in transitioning from analog workflows to digital workflows was Google Apps for Education. Initially, this was not the case during my work at Burlington. At the time of the iPad launch, Google had not developed standalone apps for iOS. Within a year, this changed. At Groton-Dunstable, students and teachers connected through shared Google Drive folders and docs. This was an efficient model along with the Google Chromebooks that students across K–12 had access to. We also turned Google Drive on for our elementary students, and turned off Gmail initially. This decision was made in order to spend some time teaching students about digital etiquette and what e-mail is.

Ultimately, students having access to Google Drive and Gmail helped significantly with the transition to digital workflows. It was also convenient that many apps integrated Google Drive. For example, teachers could post work in a shared Google Drive folder, and students could download it through an app like Notability, annotate on it, and then submit it back to the teacher. Additionally, many teachers posted resources on a Google Site or Blog that students could access PDF versions of documents that teachers wanted to share. Overall, this transition took time and support from the tech team, but eventually it created green, efficient classrooms.

HOW WERE ADMINISTRATORS PREPARED FOR THIS MAJOR CULTURE SHIFT?

In both experiences, the school and central office administrative teams were not only supportive of these initiatives, but they led the way in shifting the thinking in their respective schools. In Burlington, Superintendent Eric Conti and then–High School Principal Patrick Larkin led the PR campaign for going 1:1 with iPads in the high school. Plus, both Larkin and Conti worked closely with the tech team and listened to and supported the suggestions of tech team members as we progressed forward with the iPad initiative.

At Groton-Dunstable, I started by listening to what each building principal wanted for his or her respective school in regard to technology integration. I also asked for a vision of how they viewed technology integration and why it was important. I also spent time in each of the schools talking with groups of teachers to get their input on how they viewed technology in the classroom and what they wanted. These conversations helped me frame a roadmap for purchasing new devices and peripheral devices for each building.

As for disciplinary actions, associate principals along with building principals upheld the Acceptable Use Policies along with the guidelines approved in the student handbook for each school. For example, there wasn't a new rule written for cyber-bullying, but rather we considered bullying, whether online or in person, an offense and students were addressed accordingly. Overall, there were limited issues with students and behaviors online and with devices. With any type of disciplinary action there needs to be consistency.

The key to this process is to have conversations with administrators and listen. It is essential that contemporary technology directors have an understanding of classroom practices and 21st-century pedagogy while also having an understanding of networks and information technology. Ultimately, when districts proceed in this manner there can be many successes.

What Happened in Those Classrooms Where Teachers Didn't Adopt the Technology?

The answer is quite simple: nothing. Technology use was not a mandate or a requirement for any teacher. Teachers maintained autonomy in their respective classrooms but were encouraged to try at least a sample of technology integration. Tech integration should never be forced. Allow the process to unfold and eventually students will want and expect more from their classroom experience. Plus, iPads and Chromebooks were not needed every day. The key here is finding a healthy balance of screen time and face time.

Similarly, we had several parents who asked to opt out of their son or daughter using technology. Again, this was always an option for parents and students. Technology was never a forced mandate. For these particular students, teachers provided hard copies of work and differentiated instruction accordingly to meet the needs of those students.

Conclusions

A 1:1 technology environment is not essential to producing exemplary students. In fact, there are many students who have come before me and who I have taught who didn't care for technology. The takeaway in all of this is that all of the stakeholders and decision makers in education should begin to think differently about how we teach and assess our students. Similarly, schools need to do everything in their power and budget to provide students and teachers with access to technology and digital resources. Having this access can help provoke passions, drive careers, and highlight great student work.

What technology integration does is disrupt the status quo. The examples I've shared from students, teachers, and administrators evidence that great things can come when you lead with an open mind, a transparent philosophy, and a healthy balance and pace of change. Adopting this philosophy will outlast most device upgrades and provide an innovative model for your school. The fact is, devices will come and go. What students learn about technology today will surely not be the same in three years. However, the impetus for this book was not to encourage expanded technology budgets so that more devices can be purchased; rather, technology, regardless of the amount integrated, can provoke dramatic changes in teaching and learning. It can also open the eyes of students to new career paths and connect them with a global think tank of contemporaries engaged in the same spaces. Personally, this book has served as not only a roadmap to disrupting the education model, but as a way of reflecting on how I arrived at this point. I'll share a story to elaborate on how my educational experience changed and evolved through the help of one book and one teacher.

In 1995, I remember reading *The Road Ahead* by Bill Gates. My father shared it with me when he was done, and I am pretty sure I read it twice. The thought of what might be was fascinating to me; however, I didn't have many options in school to support this type of passion. After reading *The Road Ahead,* I wanted to be Bill Gates. I wanted to develop software and create programs that would change the future, but there were no makerspaces[1] or coding classes. The wave was just forming.

The closest I came was a Microsoft Office class where I learned how to save a file and regularly got in trouble for double-clicking the Internet Explorer icon during class. At home, around the same time I finished *The Road Ahead,* our family got a new computer that included a 14.4k modem. I'll never forget watching the first website load slowly down the screen, and how I had no idea what impact this novel moment would have on my career and the world. At that moment, I was full of questions and excited at the endless possibilities I could dream up. I'd like to think that book and the access to an early version of the Internet launched my inquisitiveness toward how things work and the possibilities of what could be. Additionally, I imagined where this device, along with the power of the Internet, could take our society.

The twist in this story is that while a book and a few pieces of hardware piqued my imagination, it was an English teacher who taught me about having a global perspective. Ms. Stellfox was a tough and stern teacher; however, underneath that facade she was gentle, caring, and soft-spoken. There were no traces of technology in her classroom, and the Socratic method of teaching was regularly employed. In essence, it was a standard classroom. However, there were elaborate stories of travel abroad that Ms. Stellfox had experienced that helped connect us to the world of Shakespeare and the Elizabethan society. While she taught us to understand and think locally, she challenged us to act globally and make broader connections.

The reason I shared this story was to show that the underlying change agent is not hardware, but it's a teacher. This teacher is dynamic and flexible in the classroom and adapts well to change—however, not just change for change's sake, but change that challenges our students and impacts their learning. This teacher is able to provide his or her students with both local and global perspectives, and find ways to engage and involve students in both of these worlds.

And this is the philosophy that we must bring into our schools every day. It's imperative that we strive to not just bring in hardware, but new paradigms for teaching and learning. And, despite the national debate over a common curriculum, it's possible to elicit creative learning opportunities for our students and still work within the parameters handed down to us in the classroom.

As I mentioned earlier, devices come and go, but dedicated, motivated teachers outlive most hardware and most applications. Education will always have its challenges, and the system is constantly changing and evolving. As districts, administrators, teachers, and parents, it is our collective job to ensure that we're providing the best access and opportunities to our students and learning with them so that their digital horizons are not blurry to us.

A while back Dean Shareski, an educational technology professor, stated that he was a giant derivative, and that it is our "moral imperative" to share.[2] After reading this book, I not only hope you share some of the ideas, but find ways to provoke a shared culture of learning and trust in your school. We are all better as a collective, and it is our job to help others on this journey. Schools can be great again and provide the groundwork for some of the best innovations in our society and throughout the world. We simply have to let it happen and plan accordingly. It is time to bring education into the 21st century and challenge our students every day. But, not just challenge them with simple recite and recall—rather, challenge them to think differently, adapt to new experiences, and occasionally embrace failure. It's time for our education system to prepare our students for their future, not ours.

I'm often asked, what's next? What will the iPad, the iPhone, and computers look like in five, 10 years? My answer is that I can only imagine. When discussed in the context of education, I refer to the first reference I shared in the introduction about the chalkboard's introduction to the classroom. Eventually, there will come a time where the iPad looks much like the individual chalk slates that students used at the end of the 19th century. My hope, in the immediate future, is that technology becomes something that we don't even notice in schools. It just happens. Ultimately, the students we teach now will decide and create what is next.

Technology does not dramatically change education; it allows us to open it up in different directions. Teachers will always teach, and dynamic pedagogy will always drive the education vehicle forward. The education field always needs experts in specified content areas that are able to adapt and innovate their practices from year to year and connect the past with the present. Essentially, what technology in education allows us to do is create broader communities from which we can all learn, share, and grow.

ENDNOTES

1. http://makerspace.com/home-page
2. https://www.youtube.com/watch?v=ELelPZWx7Zs

Appendix of Resources

District Vision for Digital Learning and Technology

It is the mission of the Groton-Dunstable Regional School District (GDRSD) to prepare students for the 21st century and the global economy. This mission is threaded throughout the fabric of our K–12 schools and developed as a literacy that all students must acquire.

To meet the needs of the 21st century learner, we must ensure students are prepared to thrive in a world that demands collaboration, innovative thinking, and adaptability. If there is one thing the 21st century as taught us, it is that nothing is certain. Our students are expected to compete in a highly competitive higher education and job market. In order to prepare students for the rigors of life beyond K–12, we must ensure that we are developing the aforementioned skills across all content areas.

In order to integrate digital learning and technology into the fabric of our school district, the GDRSD tech team will design, develop, and support a digital learning plan for each grade level. This plan will be collectively developed by the tech team and serve as a blueprint for integrating digital learning strategies that directly impact teaching and learning. The standards and goals embedded in this plan will be a collection of resources from the International Society for Technology in Education (ISTE), Massachusetts State Standards for Technology, and the Common Core State Standards.

Ultimately, this plan will be carried out by the tech team and integrated by the dynamic educators throughout the district. And, while both this vision and plan directly serves our students, it reminds every educator in the district that we are all lifelong learners who share in this process. The hope is to continually assess our work and reflect on this mission for digital learning and technology integration and to provide the best access and opportunities for our students and teachers. In order to provide our students with the most current technologies, we must continually assess our infrastructure, hardware, and software applications.

This mission, along with the mission and vision of our district, will serve to ensure that every student exhibits a desire to learn beyond our halls, which will ultimately yield an opportunity for students to graduate college and be career ready.

USES OF DIGITAL LEARNING PLAN

The GDRSD EdTech Team anticipates several specific uses for the 2020 Vision for Digital Learning in Groton-Dunstable Regional School District. The comprehensive plan provides:

- a roadmap for decision-makers to implement PK–12 digital learning in Groton-Dunstable Regional School District;

- a resource for faculty and staff to use when developing and integrating their digital learning curriculum, including alignment to best emerging practices in instructional content and assessment;

- a roadmap for the director of Technology to use in making strategic decisions district-wide regarding resource allocation and implementation; and

- specific targets for the Groton-Dunstable Regional School District School Committee to aim their resources in pursuit of the goals set out in the plan.

VISION FOR DIGITAL LEARNING COMPONENTS

Groton-Dunstable Regional School District is committed to providing students and teachers with access and opportunities to a variety of learning tools and applications. It is our goal to provide our staff and students with digital components and hardware that meets the needs of the 21st century learner. These skills help our students develop a desire for lifelong learning, constant inquiry and exploration, and responsible citizenship. In order to deliver these outcomes the Groton-Dunstable Regional EdTech team, along with school administration and faculty, will strive to provide our students and teachers with access to 21st century learning tools and applications. GDRSD is working to create a learning environment based on seamless inclusion of technology in classroom instruction and school management. Technology is no longer an add-on component or an elective; rather, it is a literacy that is threaded through the fabric of our schools.

Digital Learning and Technology Goals

Groton-Dunstable Regional School District is committed to providing, assessing, and developing a rich curriculum that includes digital learning opportunities and access to new and emerging technologies. Ultimately, it is our mission to carry out our vision for digital learning and technology and to provide our students with the skills needed to succeed in our schools, in college, and in their careers. In order to provide this environment throughout our district each year, we must present goals to serve as a roadmap for all technology integration specialists, IT managers, and library media specialists to carry out.

- Provide a robust infrastructure that is regularly assessed and upgraded.
- Provide current, acceptable hardware for teachers and students to use daily in the classroom.
- Provide access to applications and software that assist students with learning and remediation.
- Develop and design professional development opportunities for teachers, students, and the community.
- Provide access to Google Apps for Education to promote district-wide collaboration and communication.
- Ensure that all students meet grade-level technology literacy standards.

- Provide and create resources for digital learning as well as digital health and wellness for all students, teachers, and parents.
- Provide a comprehensive student information system that coordinates student data and information.
- Provide digital and non-digital library resources for research and inquiry.
- Provide support and maintenance on all district-wide software and servers.
- Align our digital literacy curriculum with the Common Core State Standards.
- Support the PARCC assessment during the pilot test and beyond.

Professional Development

It is the goal of the GDRSD tech team to provide daily support, after-school workshops, and community workshops. One of the goals of the Vision for Digital Learning and Technology is to support and educate the faculty and staff, but also educate and inform the community about our initiatives.

Daily Support
Instructional Technology Specialists

- The instructional technology specialists at the middle school and high school provide daily support for faculty, staff, and students. It is the common goal of the

(Continued)

instructional technology specialists to provide consistent support for integrating new digital learning strategies, digital resources, and assistive technologies. Along with our instructional technology specialists, the library media specialists provide students with a functioning library as well as access to digital and analog resources that help students drive research.

Network Managers

- While the instructional technology specialists focus on integrating digital learning tools and application into the classroom, it is the job of the network managers to support and maintain our infrastructure throughout the school district. It is the common goal of the network managers to ensure the network is working effectively, the servers are stable, and that the hardware inventory is working properly. The demands of this job can hardly fit one page, but their work helps ensure that our infrastructure, and our major utility, is consistently functioning to capacity.

Student Information Systems Manager

- The student information systems (SIS) manager is responsible for all of our data and state reporting

throughout the district. This position not only reports data, but he or she ensures the accuracy of all student information throughout the district. This includes grade books, GPA information, and student information data. The SIS manager develops integration strategies for current software used for reporting, and provides consistent professional development for faculty and staff.

The GDRSD EdTech Genius Bar

The GDRSD EdTech team provides a weekly, optional professional development opportunity called the EdTech Genius Bar. This event consists of two or three scheduled, focused sessions as well as general help and assistance with device maintenance. The tech team and faculty run sessions each week on a variety of topics that include apps designed for teaching and learning, hardware functionality, digital organization strategies and workflows, and so on. Weekly sessions are designed to provide the attendees with something they can immediately integrate into his or her classroom.

Community Tech Night

The Community Tech Night is held once a month at the GDRHS library and offers a variety of talks designed to showcase and educate the greater community on how we are integrating technology and provides a chance for community members to engage in workshop sessions. Sessions are presented collectively by the GDRSD EdTech team and recorded by the Groton New Channel for archiving. This monthly event is our way of being transparent with the community and how we are integrating technology, but it also serves as our way of giving back to a supportive community.

Digital Support

The GDRSD EdTech team has and continues to work collaboratively to build the GDRSD EdTech Commons. This site is built using a Google Site and allows all tech team members to add content and update information consistently. The resource is available to the entire district and the Groton-Dunstable community. All of the applications we use throughout the district can be found here, along with printed and video tutorials.

Response to Intervention (RTI)

Technology reinforces the three RTI elements—the Assessment process, Tiers of intervention, and the problem-solving process—through the utilization of Web 2.0 tools that ensure collaboration among educators, centralize resources into repositories that are accessible and affordable, and provide tracking systems for managing implemented interventions and their effects based on progress monitoring measures.

Assistive Technology

Assistive technology is integrated throughout the Groton-Dunstable Regional School District. It is the goal of the GDRSD EdTech team to provide support and accommodations for students and teachers needing to integrate technology applications and hardware to assist in the learning process. GDRSD is committed to providing a variety of hardware and digital applications for teachers and students.

Hardware:

Google Chromebook
Interactive Whiteboard
Apple TV and Flat Panel
iPad 2
Projectors
Speakers
Headphones
Microphones

Access to Digital Resources

The Policy Committee supports the right of students, employees, and community members to have reasonable access to various information formats and believes it is incumbent upon users to utilize this privilege in an appropriate manner.

SAFETY PROCEDURES AND GUIDELINES

The superintendent, in conjunction with the director of Technology, shall develop and implement appropriate procedures to provide guidance for access to digital resources. Guidelines shall address teacher supervision of student computer or tablet use, ethical use of digital resources, and issues of privacy versus administrative review of electronic files and communications. In addition, guidelines shall prohibit the use of district networks for illegal activities and for the use of other programs with the potential of damaging or destroying programs or data.

Internet safety measures shall be implemented that effectively address the following items:

- controlling access by minors to inappropriate matter on the Internet as defined by the Children's Internet Protection Act (CIPA) and the Children's Online Privacy Protection Act (COPPA);

- safety and security of minors when they are using e-mail, instant messaging applications, and other forms of direct electronic communications;

- preventing unauthorized access, including hacking, viruses, and other unlawful activities by minors online; and

- unauthorized disclosure, use, and dissemination of personal information regarding minors.

The Groton-Dunstable Regional School District shall provide reasonable public notice of, and at least one public hearing or meeting to address and communicate its Internet safety measures.

EMPOWERED DIGITAL USE

All students and faculty must agree to and sign our Empowered Digital Use form prior to the student or staff member being granted independent access to digital resources and district networks. The required form, which specifies guidelines for using district digital resources and district networks, must be signed by the parent or legal guardian of minor students (those under 18 years of age) and also by the student. This document shall be kept on file as a legal, binding document. In order to modify or rescind the agreement, the student's parent or guardian (or the student who is at least 18 years old) must provide the director of Technology with a written request.

EMPLOYEE USE

Employees shall use district e-mail, district devices, and district networks only for purposes directly related to educational and instructional purposes.

COMMUNITY USE

On recommendation of the superintendent, in conjunction with the director of Technology, the committee shall determine when and which computer equipment, software, and information access will be available to the community. All guests will be prompted to, and must accept, our district's Empowered Digital Use Policy before accessing our district network.

DISREGARD OF RULES AND RESPONSIBILITY FOR DAMAGES

Individuals who refuse to sign required Empowered Digital Use Policy documents or who violate district rules governing the use of district technology or networks shall be subject to loss or restriction of the privilege of using equipment, software, information access systems, and network.

Individuals shall reimburse the committee for repair or replacement of the district property that is lost, stolen, damaged, or vandalized while under their care.

POLICY FOR USE OF STUDENT INFORMATION AND IMAGES FOR EDUCATIONAL PURPOSES

Groton-Dunstable Regional School District attempts to provide students with the best educational resources and practices. GDRSD also seeks to recognize student achievement and success by publishing student names and/or pictures in the newspaper, district website and blogs, school newsletters, and video/cable access television. The information that may be released for publication includes only the student's name, class, participation in officially recognized activities and sports, degrees, honors, and awards. Photographs may also be taken during school activities for use on Groton-Dunstable Regional School District web pages, blogs, teacher websites, newsletters, yearbooks, and newspaper articles.

We understand that parents may not want students' names, photos, or achievements published. Parents may opt out of the use of this information for publication.

Please read the information below, sign where indicated, and return to your child's school.

Consent form for use of Images and Video for Educational Purposes

☐ YES, I give permission for Groton-Dunstable Regional School District to photograph, film, or audio record my child for use in district-approved publications, web pages, and school-related video productions and performances. This information may also be released to local news media.

☐ NO, I do not give permission for Groton-Dunstable Regional School District to photograph, film, or audio record my child for publication.

Student Name (Print) _____

Parent or Guardian Name (Print) _____

Parent or Guardian Signature _____ Date _____

INTERNET SAFETY CONSENT FORM

The Groton-Dunstable Regional School District attempts to provide students with access and opportunities to the best educational resources available. Many of these resources now take on a digital format. Many of our teachers have started incorporating web-based, digital applications and sites to enhance student learning, engagement with the curriculum, and collaboration amongst peers. Through the use of these digital tools, students and teachers can expand the classroom by participating in collaborative practices that enable students to learn appropriate and responsible ways to use the Internet. These practices provide both an exceptional educational opportunity for our academic areas as well as an opportunity to enhance student awareness and efficacy with digital tools.

The Children's Online Privacy Protection Act (COPPA) requires that parents of children under the age of 13 provide written consent for accessing and using online services. Parents of any GDRSD student may opt out of student use of these web-based applications in school.

Please read the information below, sign where indicated, and return to your child's school.

Internet Safety Consent Form and Acceptable Use

☐ **YES,** I give permission for my child to use web-based applications and open source content for the purpose of educational practices and collaboration.

☐ **NO,** I do not give permission for my child to used web-based applications during school or for educational practices and collaboration.

Student Name (Print) _____

Parent or Guardian Name (Print) _____

Parent or Guardian Signature _____

GDRSD Internet Empowered Digital Use Guidelines for Students K–8

The Internet is a wonderful resource for educational resources and experiences for students. At the same time, many websites and images are inappropriate for children of younger ages to view. Our responsibility as educators requires that we incorporate online resources in our curriculum. The purpose of this document is to make students and parents aware of the school district policies toward Internet use. This version is written with elementary and middle school students in mind. Parents, please read the contents of this policy to your children in terms they will understand, explain that by signing the form they agree to follow these rules, ask them to sign it, and sign it yourself, as well. This agreement will remain in effect as long as your child is in grades K–8. Any student without a signed Internet Acceptable Use Policy agreement will not be allowed to use computers in the Groton-Dunstable Regional School District (GDRSD).

RULES FOR USING THE INTERNET

1. Acceptable Use:

   - I will only use websites that are appropriate for children at my age level.

   - I will not copy material and say that I wrote it myself.

   - I know that inappropriate use of our school computers will break school rules and sometimes even break the law.

2. Privileges:

   - Using the Internet at school is a privilege, and my teacher and the principal make the decision whether I may use it or not. If my behavior online is inappropriate, I may lose this privilege.

3. Manners

   - I will not send mean or hurtful messages.

   - I will use appropriate language at all times.

   - I will never use another's thoughts or ideas and call them my own.

4. Online Safety

   - When I am on the Internet, I will never give out personal information about myself or anyone else (such as my name, address, town I live in, telephone number, parents' work address or work phone number, passwords, or even the name of my school).

- If I am ever upset by something I see on the Internet, I will tell an adult immediately.

- If I ever get an e-mail/instant message (IM) that is mean or frightening, I will tell an adult immediately.

- I will only use the Internet at school when a teacher or another adult is present.

5. Respect

- I will not cause any damage to school computers.

- I will not change or delete files that belong to anyone else.

- I will not give my password to anyone else, nor will I use anyone else's password.

- I will only use e-mail for school-related communication.

- I will not send harassing e-mail messages or content.

- I will not send offensive e-mail messages or content.

- I will not send spam e-mail messages or content.

- I will not send or read e-mail at inappropriate times, such as during class instruction.

- I will not send e-mail to share test answers or promote cheating in any way.

- I will not use the account of another person.

EXPECTATION OF PRIVACY

At any time and without prior notice, GDRSD reserves the right to monitor, inspect, copy, review, and store any and all usage of the network and the Internet, as well as any information sent or received in connection with this usage. Because files remain the property of GDRSD, no one should have any expectation of privacy regarding such materials.

This agreement is to be signed by students upon entering Kindergarten in the Groton-Dunstable Regional School District and will remain in effect through Grade 8.

I understand and agree to follow these rules.

_____

Student Signature   Date

I have read the GDRSD Internet/Network Acceptable Use Policy, and I approve of my child's participation in Internet/networking activities in the Groton-Dunstable schools.

_____

Parent Signature   Date

GROTON-DUNSTABLE REGIONAL SCHOOL DISTRICT EMPOWERED DIGITAL USE GUIDELINES FOR TECHNOLOGY AND NETWORKS—HIGH SCHOOL (9–12) STUDENT AGREEMENT FORM

Name (please print):_____

INTRODUCTION

On the school network and on the Internet you may participate in a variety of activities that support learning. With access to other networks and people around the world, you might have access to information that may not be appropriate. The Groton-Dunstable Regional School District has taken measures to prevent access to inappropriate information. However, we cannot control all the information available on the Internet. The district is not responsible for other people's actions or the quality and content of information available through this service. We trust our students to know what is appropriate and inappropriate based on stated school guidelines.

The following guidelines are intended to help you use the network appropriately. If you do not follow our use policies listed here, your privilege of using the network may be withdrawn.

USER AGREEMENT

The use of school and district networks must be in support of education, research, and the educational goals and objectives of the Groton-Dunstable Regional School District. You are personally responsible for this provision at all times when using building and district networks.

- The use of another organization's networks or computing resources must comply with rules appropriate to that network.

- Transmission of any material in violation of any United States statute is prohibited. This includes, but is not limited to, copyrighted material, threatening or obscene material, or material protected by trade secret.

Be familiar with these rules and how to use the Internet before getting online. If you have any questions about these rules, please ask your teacher so you can understand. Be aware that the inappropriate use of electronic information resources can be a violation of school rules, or local, state, and federal laws, and that you can be prosecuted for violating those laws.

PRIVILEGES

The use of building and district information systems is a privilege, not a right, and inappropriate use may result in a cancellation of those privileges. The district administration will decide what is appropriate, and their decision is final.

STUDENT CONDUCT

Students are expected to conduct themselves according to generally accepted rules of network/computer etiquette. Any student found to be in violation of the rules of conduct may be denied access to computers and the Internet. These rules include, but are not limited to:

- **BE POLITE:** Never send, or encourage others to send, abusive messages.

- **USE APPROPRIATE LANGUAGE:** You are a representative of your school and your district on a public system. Never swear or use vulgarities, including any other inappropriate language.

- **PRIVACY:** Do not reveal your home address, phone number, names or addresses of family members, or the addresses or phone numbers of other students or colleagues. Note that electronic mail (e-mail) is not private. People who operate the district's computer systems have access to all e-mail, and any messages relating to or in support of illegal activities may be reported to the authorities.

- **E-MAIL:** Groton-Dunstable Regional School District provides faculty, staff, and students with a Google Apps for Education account.

USES FOR STUDENT GMAIL

E-mail can be a powerful communication tool for students to increase communication and collaboration.

- Students are encouraged to check their e-mail at least once per day.

- Teachers may send e-mail to their students to communicate reminders, course content, pose questions related to class work, and such.

- Students may send e-mail to their teachers with questions or comments regarding class.

- Students may send e-mail to other students to collaborate on group projects and assist with school classes.

- **DISRUPTIONS:** Do not use the network in any way that would disrupt the use of the network by others.

- **REPRESENTATION:** Do not send anonymous messages or represent a message to have been written by another. All correspondence should be clearly identifiable as to its originator.

- **INAPPROPRIATE MATERIAL:** On a global network, it is impossible to control the content of data and an industrious user may discover inappropriate material. It is the user's responsibility not to initiate access to materials or online games that are considered to be inconsistent with educational goals, objectives, and policies. Use of inappropriate material may result in disciplinary action.

- **FILES:** Tampering with another student's files, folders, or work stored on a computer or external disk is considered trespassing and may result in disciplinary action.

- **DOWNLOADS:** Students are not allowed to download, install, or run software from the Internet onto school computers. Doing so will result in disciplinary action.

- **Non-GDRSD Devices:** Students are also encouraged to bring in their own computing devices to school for learning.

SECURITY

If you identify a security problem in the building or district networks, notify a staff member at once. Never demonstrate the problem to other users. Never use another individual's account. Never tell anyone else your password. Any user identified as a security risk will be denied access to the network and may be liable for disciplinary action or prosecution.

VANDALISM

Vandalism is defined as any malicious attempt to physically deface, disable, or destroy computers, peripherals, or other network hardware or to harm or destroy data of another user or any other agencies or networks that are connected to the system. This includes, but is not limited to, the creation or transmission of computer viruses or hacking. Any vandalism will result in loss of network privileges, disciplinary action, or possible legal referral.

This agreement is to be signed upon entering the high school and will remain in force until the student has either graduated or left the school district.

Student:

I have read the Groton-Dunstable Regional School District's policy and regulation regarding my use of the district's computer systems and the Internet. I understand my responsibilities and the consequences if I misuse the district's computer systems or use the Internet or e-mail in an inappropriate manner. I will report any observed or suspected misuse of the district's computer systems to a teacher.

Printed Name _____

Signature _____ Date _____

Parent:

I have read the Groton-Dunstable Regional School District's policy and regulation regarding my child's use of the district's computer systems and the Internet. I understand his/her responsibilities and the consequences if he/she misuses the district's computer systems or uses the Internet or e-mail in an inappropriate manner.

Printed Name _____

Signature _____ Date _____

References

CIPA. (n.d.). Unmasking the Truth collaborative wiki. Retrieved from http://unmaskdigitaltruth.pbworks.com/w/page/7254086/cipa

Sending email (K–2). (n.d.). Common Sense Media. Retrieved from https://www.commonsensemedia.org/educators/lesson/sending-email-k-2

Education.cu-portland.edu. (1960). The history of the classroom blackboard. Concordia University–Portland Online. Retrieved from http://education.cu-portland.edu/blog/reference-material/the-history-of-the-classroom-blackboard/

Fischer, K. (2014). A college degree sorts job applicants, but employers wish it meant more. *The Chronicle of Higher Education.* Retrieved from http://chronicle.com/article/A-College-Degree-Sorts-Job/137625/#id=overview

Forsyth.k12.ga.us. (2013). Responsible use guidelines for Forsyth County Schools' community. Retrieved from http://www.forsyth.k12.ga.us/responsibleuse

Friedman, T. L. (2014, February 22). How to get a job at Google. *The New York Times.* Retrieved from http://www.nytimes.com/2014/02/23/opinion/sunday/friedman-how-to-get-a-job-at-google.html?_r=0

Hu, W. (2011, September 28). A call for opening up web access at schools. *The New York Times.* Retrieved from http://www.nytimes.com/2011/09/29/education/29banned.html?_r=3&

The Hunger Games reaches another milestone: Top 10 censored books. (2008, September 26). Retrieved from http://entertainment.time.com/2011/01/06/removing-the-n-word-from-huck-finn-top-10-censored-books/slide/the-catcher-in-the-rye-2/

Iasevoli, B. (2013, December 18). After bungled iPad rollout, lessons from LA put tablet technology in a time out. *Hechinger Report.* Retrieved from http://hechingerreport.org/content/after-bungled-ipad-rollout-lessons-from-la-put-tablet-technology-in-a-time-out_14123/

Lehmann, C. (2009, February 28). *Chris Lehmann: School tech should be like oxygen.* Retrieved from https://www.youtube.com/watch?v=RUWzQYLqLLg

Shearer, A. (2012, August 3). iPads innovate education in Massachusetts schools. *The Phoenix.* http://thephoenix.com/boston/life/142238-ipads-innovate-education-in-massachusetts-schools/

Turkle, S. (2011). *Alone together.* New York, NY: Basic Books.

Ward, V. (2013, April 21). Toddlers becoming so addicted to iPads they require therapy. *The Telegraph.* Retrieved from http://www.telegraph.co.uk/technology/10008707/Toddlers-becoming-so-addicted-to-iPads-they-require-therapy.html

Index

Digital health and wellness:
  building classroom community for,
      37–41, 42–43
  digital citizenship for, 33–37, 39, 42
  federal policies and, 8, 20, 31–33
  fundamentals for, 44–45
  in GDRSD goals, 115
  pace of technology integration for, 44
  See also Federal laws; Safety
Digital learning, 2, 29, 80
  Groton-Dunstable District vision for,
      113–117
  See also Learning goals and objectives;
      Technology integration
Digital literacy:
  course on, 55–56
  digital citizenship and, 36
  in GDRSD vision statement, 115
  and living without Facebook, 40
  and the "Why?" of technology
      integration, 5
  See also Information literacy;
      Technology literacy
Digital media, 12, 36, 44. *See also* Social
  media
Digital spaces:
  and connected educators, ideas for,
      81–89
  and digital citizenship, 33–37
Digital workflows, transition to, 6, 108–109
Disciplinary actions, 109, 127. *See also*
    Acceptable use policies (AUPs);
    Inappropriate use of technology
Discovery:
  systems that foster, 68
  time allowed for, 50
Discussion thread, in building classroom
  community, 39, 40 (figure)
Disruption:
  of the education model, 111
  the mounted chalkboard as, 91
  of network users, 126
  of professional development by
      EdCamp Philly, 57
  of the status quo by technology
      integration, 110
Distractions, myths and questions about,
  94, 107
Driver's education concept, 13, 37, 45
Dropbox, 95, 101, 108
Duncan, Arne, 85, 87

Economic issues. *See* Budgeting; Global
  economy; Jobs and employment
Edcamps:
  the best technology integration at, 89
  for connecting educators, 76, 86, 88–89
  designed and carried out by students,
      64–65
  Google Hangouts and, 88
  learning and doing at, 47
  as a professional development model,
      10, 48–49
  See also NTcamps for new teachers
EdCampxEDU, 64–65
EdTech integration. *See* Technology
  integration
Edutopia, x, 81
Elementary grades:
  building classroom community in, 39
  devices not taken home from, 107
  e-mail in, 34, 35, 109
  Empowered Digital Use Guidelines for,
      122–124
  student help desk applicable in, 73
  teaching digital citizenship in, 34, 36
E-mail:
  acceptable use policies on, 9
  blogs tied to, 82, 84
  Gmail for, 51, 101, 109, 126
  introduction of, in elementary grades,
      34, 35, 109
  Mailbox app for management of, 101
  privacy and, 126
  respect in use of, 123
  safety in use of, 118
  transition to K-12 student accounts
      for, 51
Employee access to digital resources,
  GDRSD statement on, 119
Employment. *See* Careers; Jobs and
  employment
Empowered Digital Use:
  GDRSD forms on, 118–119, 124, 128
  GDRSD guidelines for, 8–9, 20,
      122–128
  See also Acceptable use policies (AUPs)
Engaged learning, 29, 47, 70
Engaging classrooms, curriculum, and
  instruction, 8, 80, 93, 94
ePubs, 61, 62, 97, 98
Equitable access, 29
Equity lease, 105

Safari browser, 80, 107
Safety:
    an MDM for, 12
    in browsing experiences, 107
    GDRSD statements on, 118, 122–123
    Internet Safety Consent form, 121
    of minors, 32, 33, 118–119
    student feeling of, 36
    in usernames, 35
    See also Digital health and wellness
SCHED.org (scheduling app), 49
School culture. *See* Cultural shift
Screens, cracked, 106. *See also* Broken
    devices
Secondary education. *See* High school
Security problems, 127. *See also*
    Inappropriate use of technology;
    Safety
Selection of devices, 6, 9–12. *See also*
    Planning
Self-directed learners, for the student help
    desk, 23, 24, 59
Shared culture of learning, 1, 47, 56, 75,
    76, 112. *See also* Cultural shift
Shareski, Dean, 86, 112
Sharing:
    blogging for, 20, 83–85
    in digital citizenship, 45
    encouragement of, 57
    finding a place for, 83–89
    as a moral imperative, 112
    no downside to sharing your work, 89
    power of, 81
    in professional development, 10, 48, 50,
        50 (figure), 52, 55
    social media for, 76, 83, 85–88
    transparency and, 20, 29
    See also Blogs and blogging;
        Collaboration; Connected educators
Sheninger, Eric, 41
ShowMe interactive whiteboard, 22, 54
Silicon Valley tech startups, classrooms
    similar to, 21
Skype, 33, 88
SmartBoard, 79, 100
Smarthistory (OER website), 98
Smartphones, 26, 33, 92, 102. *See also*
    Cellphones; iPhones; Mobile phones
Snapchat, 107
Social media:
    blocking of, 31, 32, 107

and building classroom community, 39
for connected educators, 76, 83, 85–88
credibility on, 67, 86
distraction of, 107
federal laws and, 31
good defense needed for, 44
lesson plan that includes, 42
parents and, 41
posting garbage on, 27
privacy rights on, 45
in professional development, 48
respect when using, 9
school policies on, 41. *See also*
        Acceptable use policies (AUPs)
for sharing, 76, 83, 85–88
stigmatization of, 77
understanding inappropriate use of, 44
See also Facebook; Hangouts (Google+
        feature); Instagram; Snapchat;
        Twitter
Spam, 123
Speed, infrastructure, 7. *See also*
        Bandwidth
Spencer, John, 40
Sports fundamentals, 44
Sprang, Julie, 37
Standardized tests, 5, 6, 29
Standard practice, alternatives to, 95–103
Standards:
    acceptable use policy aligned with, 8
    CCSS. *See* Common Core State
        Standards (CCSS)
    of digital citizenship, 37
    in GDRSD vision statement, 113
    integrated into K-12 student
        preparation, 34
Stealing of information, 35. *See also*
        Acknowledgment of others' ideas and
        work; Copyright
Stellfox, Mrs. (English teacher), 111
Stolen property, 119
Student help desk:
    course description for, 60–63
    EdCampxEDU and, 64–65
    Google Hangouts used by, 87–88
    interview process for, 23 (figure), 23–24,
        59–60
    pathways for student helpers, 61–62
    professional development and, 49, 57
    results and impact of, 63–64, 73
    as a support system, 13, 59